YORK NOTES

General Editors: Professor A.N. Jeffares (*University of Stirling*) & Professor Suheil Bushrui (*A— University of Beirut*)

William G____ng

LORD OF
THE FLIES

Notes by Alastair Niven

MA (CAMBRIDGE) MA (GHANA) PHD (LEEDS)
Director-General, The Africa Centre, London
Honorary Lecturer, University of London

LONGMAN
YORK PRESS

YORK PRESS
Immeuble Esseily, Place Riad Solh, Beirut.

LONGMAN GROUP UK LIMITED
Longman House, Burnt Mill, Harlow,
Essex CM20 2JE, England
and Associated Companies throughout the World.

© Librairie du Liban 1980

All rights reserved. No part of this publication may be reproduced,
stored in a retrieval system, or transmitted in any form or by any
means, electronic, mechanical, photocopying, recording, or otherwise,
without the prior permission of the copyright owner.

First published 1980
Fifth impression 1986

ISBN 0-582-78100-0 .

Produced by Longman Group (FE) Ltd
Printed in Hong Kong

Contents

Part 1

Introduction

WILLIAM GOLDING is one of those writers whose first novel secured him a lasting fame and who, as a result, has been trying to escape from its reputation ever since. *Lord of the Flies* was first published in 1954. The firm which published it was Faber and Faber, among whose directors was the poet and essayist T. S. Eliot: a publishing firm with a reputation for intellectual fastidiousness. Golding at the time was a schoolmaster at Bishop Wordsworth's School in Salisbury. He was leading the active but unremarkable life of a teacher in a small cathedral city in the south of England. Faber took the script of his first novel because they recognised how successfully it caught the mood of post-war Europe when people seriously questioned if there could ever be a lasting peace again. More fundamentally, they wondered if the human race could come to terms with the new knowledge it had gained as the result of splitting the atom. It was against the background of this uncertainty that *Lord of the Flies* was conceived. It dealt with complex issues of morality and philosophy, but did so in the manner of a boy's adventure story, or a fable, or an allegory: elements of all three coexist in the novel. Golding caught the tenor of the early 1950s so successfully that his novel was quickly established as one of the most influential as well as fashionable books of its decade.

Lord of the Flies became, as much as any work can in its author's lifetime, an instant classic: Penguin Books in fact included it in their list of Modern Classics. It has never gone out of print, it has been among the best-selling novels in post-war Britain, it has been studied in schools and universities all over the world, and it has been the subject of an award-winning film by the distinguished director Peter Brook. All this attention has inevitably had two adverse effects. First, the novel's detractors have insisted that its 'cult' reputation is undeserved, that its modish theme conceals too facile and glib a comprehension of the problems it discusses. Secondly, the extraordinary interest the book has aroused undoubtedly led to expectations for his later work which Golding was not prepared to fulfil. While his subsequent works have been the subject of theses and learned articles it is true to say that nothing written by Golding since *Lord of the Flies* has had the same impact on society or as wide a readership.

In Part 3 of this study we shall examine the reputation of *Lord of the Flies* critically to see whether it has indeed been overpraised or whether it deserves its general reputation as a contemporary classic. For the moment, let us think about it in the context of Golding's career as a whole. Golding was born on 19 September 1911 and educated at Marlborough Grammar School in Wiltshire. Though almost all his life has been lived in this prosperous farming county of southern England, Golding does not possess a strong regional character in his writing. If we compare him with Thomas Hardy, from the neighbouring area of Dorset, we can see how environmentally neutral his novels tend to be. In *Lord of the Flies*, when the boys dream of England it is true that they think of country cottages and cream teas of the kind most people associate with Golding's own part of the country, but in none of his work does he appear to make Wiltshire characteristics essential to the basic conception.

The simple facts about Golding's life do not differ, in the early years, from those of hundreds of middle-class school-teachers like him. After his schooling he went to Brasenose College in the University of Oxford. Years later, in 1966, when he was a well established author, Brasenose elected him to an Honorary Fellowship. Later, in 1970, the new University of Sussex awarded him an honorary doctorate. These academic honours came to him because of his distinction as a writer, but from 1945 to 1961 he was working with great success as a teacher of classics and related arts subjects at Bishop Wordsworth's School. This is a 'public school' to which, despite its name, only fee-paying and therefore relatively privileged boys are sent. In common with most of the English public schools (until very recently, at least) it caters only for one sex and it has strong associations with the Church of England. These points matter when we come to examine *Lord of the Flies* closely. Golding creates the novel partly out of an understanding of juvenile psychology. As we see in Part 3, the boys who come to the island tend, with the exception of Piggy, to be well-spoken and strangely protected from any sordid knowledge of society. A pack of slum children bombed out of the East End of London, where some of the poorest Londoners live and where great damage was inflicted in the Second World War, might behave differently.

Lord of the Flies (1954) has been followed by six more novels, some short stories, a collection of essays, a play, and three novellas under the collective title *The Scorpion God* (1971). None of these works is very long, for Golding's accuracy of perception does not need an epic scale to sustain it. *The Inheritors*, which was published in the year after *Lord of the Flies*, immediately made it clear that Golding would not be content to repeat the same form or to take the easy option of creating the same kind of allegory in another exotic setting. The narrative technique is more opaque, with none of the sharp outlines of plot and characterisation displayed in the first book. Once again we have an isolated group of people, but the Neanderthal men in *The Inheritors* are prehistoric: that is, isolated from social history in a way fundamentally different from the boys in *Lord of the Flies*. It is impossible to read *Lord of the Flies* without being aware of the outside world—the dead parachutist on the hill embodies it and the regression to 'savagery' means something to us only if we contrast it with the 'civilisation' from which the boys lapse. In *The Inheritors*, however, the Neanderthal characters live an entirely sensuous existence, without knowledge beyond the physical life, pure innocents of a kind which any reader of *Lord of the Flies* will see to be untrue of the boys right from the start.

Pincher Martin (1956) continues the archetypal motifs that were evident in the first two novels. The protagonist here is a castaway upon a rock in the middle of the Atlantic Ocean. Golding has always liked to cross-refer to other works of literature in his fiction. In *Lord of the Flies* the most obvious source is R. M. Ballantyne's *The Coral Island* (see Part 3), first published in 1858. In *The Inheritors* connections can be drawn with H. G. Wells's historical writings and with J. R. Tolkien's *Lord of the Rings*. The connections that *Pincher Martin* suggests are more imposing: Defoe's *Robinson Crusoe* most obviously, but also traditional legends, stories from the Bible like that of Jonah, and both Greek and Shakespearean tragedy.

Golding's work in recent years has become more concerned than ever with the difficult analysis of the process of understanding itself. He attempts not just to perceive the truths of human life but to inquire into the essence of perception as an act we undertake. Inevitably, therefore, his fiction has become more concentrated, possibly more abstract in appearance, certainly more symbol-filled. *Free Fall* (1959) and *The Spire* (1964) extend the themes of the earlier books, suggesting that Golding's fascination with the recesses of man's nature has not yet been exhausted. In particular a mythic element, only implicit in *Lord of the Flies*, predominates in these later works. The same is true of *The Pyramid* (1969). In 1979, after a long silence, Golding's complex fable *Darkness Visible* was published.

Golding's play, *The Brass Butterfly*, was based on a long-short story he had written earlier, entitled 'Envoy Extraordinary', which forms one of the trilogy eventually published as *The Scorpion God*. It was dramatised at the request of the late Alastair Sim, one of Britain's most distinguished comic actors, and presented at the Strand Theatre, London, in 1958. It ran for only a month and its failure did not encourage Golding to write again for the theatre. The play has a Roman setting, and in this respect continues its author's involvement with ancient societies. Something of this interest in the classical past especially is expressed in the 'occasional pieces' which compose *The Hot Gates* (1965). The essay of chief interest in this collection, however, must always be 'Fable', which Golding based on a lecture he gave in America in 1962. In it he 'answered some of the standard questions which students were asking' about *Lord of the Flies.*

Golding wrote *Lord of the Flies* at a time of great uncertainty in world affairs. The Second World War, culminating in the explosion over Hiroshima and Nagasaki of the A-bombs, had been over only nine years. Since then there had been almost constant eruptions of violence all over the world: the partitions of Korea and India, the establishment of Israel, the nationalist agitation against the French in Indo-China, all continued the uncertainties of the previous decade. Colonial government was in retreat throughout the world. Eastern Europe had been divided from the West by what Winston Churchill termed the 'Iron Curtain'. In America there was a systematic rooting-out of the Communist 'menace'. Extremism of all sorts threatened the survival of all forms of political administration. Intellectually, too, the aftermath of Existentialism, a philosophical school of thought which denied the validity of God and proposed the hopelessness of man's condition, led to statements of great pessimism in literature. *Lord of the Flies* was written within a year or two of Albert Camus' *The Rebel* (1952) and Samuel Beckett's *Waiting For Godot* (1953), two works that similarly seek to distil an essential disturbance which the authors see at the kernel of human nature.

In setting his novel on a tropical island Golding takes *The Coral Island* as his immediate model. *Lord of the Flies* both extends and parodies Ballantyne's book. The tradition for using an island as the setting for archetypal depictions of man's state goes back at least as far as the *Philoctetes* of Sophocles. In the notes to each chapter one or two connections with Shakespeare's last play, *The Tempest*, are suggested, for Ralph emulates Prospero in certain limited ways by trying to rule an island by methods that contradict its primeval natural harmony. *Robinson Crusoe* (1719), and R. L. Stevenson's *Treasure Island* (1883), which are both mentioned in the text, come to mind when we read *Lord of the Flies*, but Golding's distinctive achievement is to have created a self-sufficient image of his own, whose debt to other influences is comparatively incidental. At the source of the book is the myth of Eden in the Book of Genesis, whereby man's first innocence is corrupted by his inability to resist sin. The myth has appealed in some way or another to writers in every generation in Christian society, but Golding manages to secularise it without destroying its viability as an illustration of the human temptation to do wrong.

William Golding must be placed in the context of his own generation, disorientated by war and by philosophic beliefs that discouraged faith in God or man. Twenty-five years later he might well have written the book in a different way for the changed political and intellectual circumstances of today. The book will last, however, because Golding transcends his own society to probe into the fundamental verities upon which he believes history itself has evolved. In Part 3 these findings are looked at closely. For the moment, some words from his lecture in *The Hot Gates* serve to remind us of how simple a writer he is, and how complex too:

> Man is a fallen being. He is gripped by original sin. His nature is sinful and his state perilous. I accept the theology and admit the triteness; but what is trite is true; and a truism can become more than a truism when it is a belief passionately held. I looked round me for some convenient form in which this thesis might be worked out, and found it in the play of children. I was well situated for this, since at the time I was teaching them. Moreover, I am a son, brother, and father. I have lived for many years with small boys, and understand and know them with awful precision. I decided to take the literary convention of boys on an island, only make them real boys instead of paper cutouts with no life in them; and try to show how the shape of the society they evolved would be conditioned by their diseased, their fallen nature. ('Fable', p.88)

A note on the text

WILLIAM GOLDING: *Lord of the Flies*, Faber & Faber, London, 1954. The book is also issued in a Faber paperback edition.

There are alternative issues of the novel less readily available than the Faber publication but a standard text is used in all of them. The choice of edition therefore does not greatly affect our study of the novel.

Part 2

Summaries
of LORD OF THE FLIES

A general summary

Lord of the Flies can be read on several levels at the same time. What follows is a chapter-by-chapter summary of the story, followed by notes to explain specific details or to direct the reader critically. A full critical examination appears in Part 3.

Whatever its intellectual pretensions, William Golding has created a successful adventure story about a group of boys abandoned on a tropical island somewhere in the Pacific Ocean. They are the victims of a war which is still raging elsewhere. Golding shows how the boys adapt to the island, learning how to make fire, to build shelters, to hunt and to maintain discipline. Initially they relish their new freedom but under the strain of their total isolation they develop tensions which finally break out into conflict. They reject their first leader, replacing him by a boy who is better able to cope with the physical hardships of the island. The community they develop around him is aggressive but also prepared to accept his absolute authority. When rescue finally comes the boys have lost all touch with the 'civilised' values of their former existence. They have become like 'savages'.

In addition to being an adventure story the novel has important dimensions morally, psychologically, anthropologically and even theologically. It can be interpreted as an allegory of the human urge to do bad. It also skilfully reworks the theme of R. M. Ballantyne's *The Coral Island*, one of a number of classic tales about islands. All these points are fully discussed in Part 3.

Detailed summaries

Chapter 1 The Sound of the Shell

Two schoolboys meet by a lagoon on what they speculate to be an un-inhabited island somewhere in the tropics. They attempt to make sense of their situation, knowing only that the aeroplane in which they were travelling has crashed on the island and the pilot has probably been killed. They assume that some of the other children on the flight must have survived but that there are almost certainly no adults ('grown-ups') anywhere near. The two boys introduce themselves to each other: one is Ralph, a handsome, active, innocent boy of twelve; the other, who is fat, unattractive and wearing glasses, confides that at school he was known as 'Piggy' but he is desperate not to be known as that now. Ralph ignores his plea, delighting in the silly nickname.

Ralph adapts quickly to his new island, plunging happily into the sea. Piggy is more cautious, afraid of his incipient asthma. The boys talk nostalgically of the homes they have left behind. Then Piggy discovers a conch shell in the lagoon and suggests to Ralph that if blown loudly it could be used to summon a meeting of the other children they believe to be scattered on the island.

Ralph blows the horn and gradually a number of boys accumulate on the beach. They are of varying ages and in various states of undress after the crash. Finally a party of choirboys, still in their cloaks and ruffs and led by a senior boy called Jack Merridew, joins the meeting.

The boys exchange names (to the humiliation of Piggy, whose nickname is revealed openly) and talk about rescue. Meanwhile they agree to elect a chief. Ralph, who is holding the conch, is elected by a clear majority over Jack. He immediately sets out with Jack and a third boy, Simon, to check if they are indeed on an island. Piggy wants to come too but is rejected by Ralph. The three 'explorers' confirm that it is an island by climbing a high hill though they keep being diverted by little games on the way. On the return journey they encounter a young pig but it escapes before they can bring themselves to slaughter it. They all feel embarrassed by their diffidence and Jack, who has already insisted on hunting for food as the main priority facing the boys, promises he will kill next time.

NOTES AND GLOSSARY:

lagoon: a stretch of salt water parted from the sea by a low sand-bank. The word immediately suggests that the story takes place somewhere in the South Pacific (partly confirmed on pp.66 and 115), but Golding is careful not to be geographically explicit

his school sweater ... his grey shirt: the boys in the novel vary in age from five (the normal age that English children start school) to about twelve. It is customary at most English schools to wear a uniform, which is often grey in colour. The fact that Ralph and the others are still wearing theirs indicates that they were travelling as an official group. Golding implies that they are evacuees from a war. As we learn later in the novel, when the dead parachutist arrives on the island, aerial conflict is still occurring

the long scar: the line traced by the crashed aircraft (possibly shot down) which has brought the boys to the island

the Home Counties: traditionally these are the counties (administrative areas) bordering on London: Surrey, Kent, Essex, Middlesex (which has ceased to exist as an official area since Golding wrote *Lord of the Flies*). Two other counties close to London are sometimes included: Hertfordshire and Buckinghamshire. The Home Counties are often equated with English middle-class respectability and a prosperous way of life

Where's the man with the megaphone?: presumably the official in charge of the boys who, like all the adults, has been killed in the crash

asthma: a respiratory disease characterised by difficult breathing and a cough. His tendency to be asthmatic makes Piggy particularly vulnerable to any kind of physical effort

specs: a colloquial abbreviation for spectacles,or glasses

them fruit: this, like most of Piggy's phrasing, is grammatically wrong. It should, of course, be 'that fruit' or 'those fruits'. Golding is indicating that Piggy is less educated than Ralph and from a less privileged social background

fledged: an unusual use of the word, which, strictly used, means 'feathered', but here Golding uses it as an image for 'fringed'

flinked: the meaning of this word is not difficult to define in the context—the surface sprays whitely as it hits the reef. There is no dictionary version of the word, however, and presumably Golding has made it up. The word appears again in Chapter 8: Jack 'flinked' his hands. Here it indicates flicking sprays of blood

my auntie: an indication that Piggy has not had quite as normal and comfortable an upbringing as Ralph. We learn that his father is dead. It is less clear what has happened to his mother, though she has possibly left him in the care of his aunt

Piggy: a typical nickname given at school to a fat or greedy boy (Piggy is interested in food throughout the novel)

whizzoh!: a piece of schoolboy slang to express enthusiasm, now sounding rather dated

sucks to your auntie!: a slang expression suggesting contempt

the atom bomb: first exploded at Hiroshima, Japan, in 1945. Golding makes it clear that there has been an atomic holocaust while the boys were in the aeroplane

here was a coral island: Ralph's musings remind us of R. M. Ballantyne's novel *The Coral Island*

moo-ed like a cow . . .: we are supposed to imagine that Piggy has been prattling on while Ralph contemplates the conch

wubber: an onomatopoeic word which matches sound and meaning: it suggests a sighing sound dying away

a black, bat-like creature: the boy's shadow, the author goes on to explain; but the bat is traditionally associated with night and the devil. Golding's image intimates the presence of evil among the children

the creature: is a party of choirboys led by Jack. Variants on this uniform of black cloaks embossed with a silver cross and topped off by a frill, or ruff, are still worn in choir schools in England, of which there are several attached to Anglican cathedrals and churches. There is something threatening about Jack's choir, however; the 'square black caps' that the boys wear may remind us of the black cap formerly assumed by the judge in a British court of law when he sentenced a prisoner to death

Gib.; and Addis: Gibraltar and Addis Ababa, capital of Ethiopia. The children seem to have passed through these places in their evacuation

matins: the morning service in an Anglican church

precentor: normally the official in an Anglican cathedral who ranks next to the dean. He is normally in charge of the musical arrangements

chapter chorister: senior member of the choir

togs: (*slang*) clothes

Wacco; Wizard; Smashing: these are all schoolboy exclamations. Today, they are slightly dated expressions

this belongs to us: Ralph's phrase, coming immediately after confirmation that they are on an island, recalls Caliban in Shakespeare's *The Tempest* (Act I, Scene ii):

> This island's mine, by Sycorax my mother,
> Which thou tak'st from me.

Ralph takes possession of the island, usurping its ownership by the natural world (for example 'the butterflies' mentioned just above), just as Prospero took the island from its inhabitant, Caliban

mountain: the small boys see it as a mountain but to the adult reader it can hardly be more than a hill since it can be climbed with comparatively little difficulty. It is typical of Golding's narrative method to ascribe the children's view to the physical world rather than to interpret it with the vocabulary of a more mature person

they always talk about sticking a pig: pig-sticking was a favourite sport in India under the British Raj. The 'they' to whom Ralph refers are the adults who have told him about the sport

---

Chapter 2 Fire on the Mountain

Ralph has called another meeting to report what he, Jack and Simon have discovered on their trip across the island. He urges the need for rules and discipline if the island is to be well managed. It may be a long time before rescue comes. The boys are excited by the prospect—it reminds them of adventure stories they have read. Jack proposes that they go hunting. A little boy mentions a snake-like beast he has seen in the woods at night and the assembly argues about whether such a thing could exist on an island. Ralph then proposes that they have a fire high up on the hill so that rescuers will see it. Everyone rushes away, including, to Piggy's disgust, Ralph, and the assembly thus comes to an abrupt end.

The boys build a pile of wood and leaves, but Ralph and Jack realise that they have no means of lighting a fire. Then, when Piggy comes on the scene, Jack has the idea of using his spectacles to create a flame by angling the sun through the lenses. Piggy protests but the plan works. Jack proposes that his choir, or 'hunters' as he now calls them, look after the fire. While everyone is debating the chances of rescue, Piggy notices that their fire has gone out of control and is sweeping the forest. Piggy's exasperation at the way no one is planning anything sensibly leads to a small quarrel between him and Ralph, but Piggy breaks off when he notices that the small child who had feared the snake-beast at their first assembly is now missing. The youngest children scream in terror of snakes and the senior boys leave unsaid their realisation that the missing child is burnt alive.

NOTES AND GLOSSARY:

we'll have to have 'hands up' like at school: Ralph recollects the discipline he has learned at school where, in order to attract attention to speak, a boy must raise his hand and ask permission

whee-oh!; wacco!; bong!; doink!: more schoolboy expressions, though this time they indicate summary justice

Treasure Island: Robert Louis Stevenson's classic adventure of piracy on a tropical island (published 1883)

Swallows and Amazons: Arthur Ransome wrote twelve books in the *Swallows and Amazons* series (published between 1930 and 1947). They are all outdoor adventure stories remarkable for their accuracy of detail and their penetrating characterisation of children

[The] Coral Island: R. M. Ballantyne's adventure novel about a tropical island (published 1858) was a favourite with Victorian boys but has kept its appeal for modern readers too (see Part 3). Many of the boys in *Lord of the Flies* would have read one or more of the three books mentioned here

he was a shrimp of a boy: he was very small

the snake-thing: this does not exist, but has been imagined by the boy in his terror at finding himself on the island

the Queen: Queen Elizabeth II came to the British throne in 1952 and *Lord of the Flies* was published in 1954. Clearly the atomic disaster which Golding envisages happening before the boys reach the island is not, therefore, historically real, since the only actual atomic explosions in wartime took place in Japan in 1945 when George VI was still king. Golding creates a likely situation that might follow an atomic war, but the situation is entirely imagined

'Like kids!' he said scornfully. 'Acting like a crowd of kids!': Piggy speaks like a middle-aged father to his children (kids)

Their black caps of maintenance: the cap of maintenance is a cap worn as a symbol of official dignity. At coronation ceremonies it is carried before the sovereign

The shameful knowledge grew in them and they did not know how to begin confession: Golding uses the language of theology (especially associated with Original Sin) to express the boys' ignorance of how to make fire

'The conch doesn't count on top of the mountain', said Jack, 'so you shut up.': Jack is already questioning the authority and discipline which has been set over him and which the conch symbolises. Whilst he has a rebellious and even anarchistic streak in him he is not altogether wrong to distinguish between symbol and practicality. He is warning the boys that they cannot depend on symbols alone if they are to survive

We're English; and the English are best at everything: Jack's unquestioning pride of race strikes an illiberal note today. The fact that Golding ascribes the remark to the aggressive and unimaginative Jack suggests that he does not endorse its sentiment, but it is worth remembering that children brought up in the cold-war atmosphere of Europe in the early 1950s were often encouraged to have stridently nationalistic views

Altos ... trebles: two groups within the choir; the altos will be older than the trebles with a deeper vocal tone

Them kids. The little 'uns ... Who knows how many we got?: Piggy's question is never answered. It is the first thing the naval officer who rescues the boys at the end of the novel wants to know, and he is disappointed that the boys have been such poor representatives of their country's intelligence that they have not even taken the basic step of counting themselves

The crowd was as silent as death: this point marks the first death in the novel. The boy with the birthmark on his face who expresses terror at the snakes (see p.39) has rushed into the woods where the spreading bush-fire has presumably burnt him alive

---

Chapter 3 Huts on the Beach

Jack penetrates the forest and tracks down a pig, but the animal escapes him. He joins Ralph, who, with Simon, is trying to build a shelter. Ralph deplores the inability of the other children to concentrate on the job in hand: they keep running off to enjoy themselves. He and Jack start quarrelling over whether shelters or meat are the greater priority for the castaways. Ralph says they need a protection against the beast of the night—not that he believes in it, of course, but the other children seem to do so. Jack admits that when he is hunting he sometimes senses another being close by—not that there is, of course! Simon, meanwhile, has wandered off, and they both agree he is a strange child.

Simon explores the forest, marvelling at the beauty and harmony of the natural world and discovering within it a secret place of his own.

NOTES AND GLOSSARY:

Here was a loop of creeper with a tendril pendant from a node: Golding's language is deliberately ornate in order to express the exoticism, even the baroque quality, of the tropical vegetation

the uncommunicative forest: through phrases like this, Golding emphasises the opposition of man and nature on the island. The boys are always intruders

littluns: this word, derived from Piggy's 'little 'uns' (little ones), now becomes the standard way in the novel of referring to the youngest children

As if it wasn't a good island: another possible echo of *The Tempest* (see p.31), though Ralph's remark contrasts with Caliban's:

> The isle is full of noises,
> Sounds, and sweet airs, that give delight,
> and hurt not. (Act III, Scene ii)

batty; crackers: schoolboy slang for 'mad'

And I work all day with nothing but Simon and you come back and don't even notice the huts!: Ralph's remark sounds very like that of an unappreciated wife to the husband who has been out at work all day. Part of Golding's allegory re-creates, and partly parodies, the domestic world the boys have left behind in Europe

He's buzzed off: schoolboy slang for 'he's gone away'

Got fed up: slang for 'become bored'

sepals: the outer leaves which encase the bud of a flower

Chapter 4 Painted Faces and Long Hair

The boys have settled into a daily routine, as much as possible adapting the daily pattern of their life in England to the tropical island they are now inhabiting. The youngest children, now called 'littluns', spend a lot of time playing, especially building decorated sand-castles. Roger, an older child, taunts one of the littluns but avoids harming him with the stones he is throwing. He joins Jack, who is smearing clay and charcoal on his face as a disguise against the pigs he wants to hunt. The mask Jack assumes gives him renewed courage, also inspiring Roger and the twins Sam and Eric.

Meanwhile Ralph, Piggy (busy making practical suggestions about constructing a sundial), Simon and an older boy called Maurice are chatting and swimming. Suddenly Ralph espies a ship on the horizon. The boys rush to the place where the fire is maintained and find that it has been allowed to go out. Ralph is in despair at the lost opportunity for rescue.

The hunters return, led by Jack, who is celebrating their first kill. Ralph laments that, though he is chief, Jack's group will not listen to what he says. In the ensuing tension Piggy speaks up for Ralph and is slapped by Jack for his pains. His spectacles fall to the ground, smashing one lens. Jack reluctantly apologises to Ralph for letting the fire go out but Ralph does not reciprocate with any courtesies. His silence wins him new respect as chief but strengthens Jack's resentment of him.

Jack and the hunters roast the pig they have killed. Ralph and Piggy are included in the feast, a minor submission to Jack on their part and a small victory on his. The hunters describe how they stalked and caught the pig. They re-enact the hunt, with Maurice taking the part of the pig. Afterwards, Ralph calls an official assembly as a matter of urgency.

NOTES AND GLOSSARY:

the first two sentences of the chapter: compare William Wordsworth, *The Prelude*, Book XI, *ll*.108–9, 'Bliss was it in that dawn to be alive,/ But to be young was very Heaven!' or Wordsworth, 'Ode: Intimations of Immortality from Recollections of Early Childhood', Stanza VII, *ll*.85–6,'Behold the Child among his new-born blisses./ A six years' Darling of a pigmy size!' Golding suggests that the children enjoy a natural innocence when they first come to the island, though the seeds of dispute grow fast

the reef over the stretch of water where the snapping sharks waited: we are reminded that the island is also a prison, surrounded by hostile natural forces against which the boys are powerless until some outside agency rescues them.

biguns: big ones, as opposed to 'littluns'

the great Pacific tide: the nearest we get to an explicit geographical placing of the island. It implies that it is somewhere in the South Seas but no indication is given of the group of islands of which it forms part

a cluster of nuts, fibrous lumps as big as rugby balls: another example of Golding's finding an image suitable to the schoolboy imagination. Roger, one of the most physical and non-intellectual of the children, is reminded by the nuts of his sporting days at school. (In rugby football the ball used is oval in shape, and about a foot long.) It is a natural extension of his thoughts for him to start pelting Henry with stones

the taboo of the old life: knowledge that throwing stones is dangerous and therefore forbidden. However, with no 'parents and school and policemen and the law' to apply the rules or to enforce punishment 'the old life' has a progressively weaker hold over Roger and the others

a civilization that knew nothing of him and was in ruins: the phrase emphasises the isolation of the boys and also reminds us of the devastation in the adult world. Roger's stone-throwing is trivial compared to the mass destruction elsewhere, but it is not hard to find the connections between his childish action and the atomic disaster which has destroyed his inheritance in the northern hemisphere

like moths on a tree trunk: Jack is explaining the need for camouflage if the hunters are to be successful in trapping a pig. Later on their use of disguise will take on a new role, ceremonial and ritual

Samneric: Sam and Eric. The identical twins do so much together that they operate virtually as one person. Hence the blending of their names

his fat body was golden brown: even Piggy (described on p.13 as 'palely and fatly naked') has been changed physically by the island surroundings

as though baldness were his natural state: this underlines Piggy's tendency to appear middle-aged. In Western culture baldness is sometimes associated with a high level of intelligence

belly flop: an unsuccessful dive into water

Oh God, oh God!: in one way this is a conventional expression (perhaps in imitation of his elders) of Ralph's frustration and anger at not knowing how to attract the attention of the passing ship. Golding surely intends us, however, to take it literally: there is an instinctive urge in man, at moments of his greatest impotence and need, to call upon God even if he has no rational conviction of His existence

Kill the pig. Cut her throat. Spill her blood: this becomes a celebratory chant repeated among the hunters at moments of high emotion

a nick in the hilt: Jack intends to cut a notch in the handle of his knife. This primitive way of recording the number of one's killings can be found in most societies

this verbal trick: Jack's apology

wetly: weakly, pathetically; nothing to do with liquid

ha'porth: a halfpenny-worth, that is, almost nothing

One for his nob!: the children are recalling the slaughter of the pig. The expression means 'hit it on the head'; 'Give him a fourpenny one!' is a colloquial way of saying 'bash it in!'

Chapter 5 Beast from Water

Evening is starting to fall. Ralph thinks hard about the assembly he has called. He knows it is important to emphasise the seriousness of their situation on the island, how jobs have been neglected while people enjoyed themselves. He wonders to himself if he has the ability to think in the right way (as Piggy, for example, can think) or if anything now has any real meaning.

The assembly starts well. Ralph reminds the boys that they have stopped collecting water, that interest in building shelters dropped off after the first one was put up, and that standards of sanitation have been neglected. He next warns them that the fire must be kept alight at all times, for it is more essential to them than hunting pigs. He decrees that the fire will always be on the hill, even if this inconveniences those people who want to use it for cooking their food. Finally he suggests that their community is beginning to fragment because of an unnamed fear which they are all, including himself, feeling from time to time. He suggests they talk about their fear to find out what it is.

Jack speaks now, insisting that there cannot be a beast because he has hunted all over the island and never seen it. He suggests that the fear they sometimes feel is only the result of nightmares.

Piggy speaks next, having to cope with some heckling as he does so. He agrees with Jack that there is no beast but he does not agree with him that their fear is only dreamt.

A littlun called Phil describes how he woke from a nightmare the previous night and saw 'something big and horrid' in the trees.

Simon tries to talk about the secret place in the woods he has discovered (see end of Chapter 3), but no one will give him a serious hearing.

A littlun called Percival has indicated something about seeing the beast but when Piggy questions him all he can do is weep. This sets the rest of the littluns crying, but Maurice manages to divert them with some clowning.

Up to this point the conch has been passed ceremonially from speaker to speaker: no one has addressed the assembly without it. Jack now breaks this 'rule'. He bullies Percival into speech and the little boy mutters that the beast came out of the sea. A disorganised chatter of possibilities follows. Simon, very shy, tries to explain to the boys that the beast may exist, not as an animal in the woods but as a state of being in themselves. No one takes him seriously and once again the assembly starts to fall apart.

Ralph tries to halt the threatened anarchy by asking who believes in ghosts, but the boys express their irrationality by voting for their existence. Piggy protests impotently. Jack tries to stop him and Ralph points out that Piggy has the conch. Jack denounces the rules, however, and destroys the assembly finally by announcing that the hunters will kill the beast.

Ralph, Piggy and Simon are left together wondering what to do, and what action grown-ups would take in their situation. The hunters can be heard assembling. Piggy points out to Ralph that Jack really hates him. Ralph longs for a sign from the adult world, while in the distant darkness Percival has another nightmare.

NOTES AND GLOSSARY:

There must be no mistake about this assembly, no chasing imaginary . . . :
Ralph is collecting his thoughts as a leader must who is called upon to defend his position before his own people

Only, decided Ralph as he faced the chief's seat, I can't think. Not like Piggy: Ralph recognises that he has the qualities of leadership but that these are useless without practical advice to sustain them. 'Piggy was no chief,' he goes on to think, but he understands that Piggy is a kind of Prime Minister to his own role as monarch. The key to Ralph's speech to the meeting comes right at the start: 'We need an assembly. Not for fun . . . But to put things straight.' He tries to make the boys face reality by reminding them that survival and eventual rescue are dependent upon the strict observance of rules and social duties

. . . if you're taken short: if you want to go to the lavatory. Ralph is the only member to be concerned about hygiene

Things are breaking up. I don't understand why. We began well; we were happy. And then—: Ralph's words are an uncomprehending child's expression of what W. B. Yeats wrote in his poem 'The Second Coming':

> Things fall apart; the centre cannot hold;
> Mere anarchy is loosed upon the world,
> The blood-dimmed tide is loosed, and everywhere
> The ceremony of innocence is drowned;
> The best lack all conviction, while the worst
> Are full of passionate intensity.

Ralph is 'the best', but his speech does not prevent the group sliding away from him, while Jack, 'the worst', wins more supporters by his sheer self-confidence and urgency

A picture of three boys walking along the bright beach flitted through his mind: Ralph recalls the expedition with Jack and Simon to find out whether they were on an island

cry-babies and sissies: schoolboy words for 'cowards'

fear can't hurt you any more than a dream: as so often with Jack, he is half right. But he has no understanding that dreams *can* hurt, because they do psychological harm. He perceives things only in a sensuous way and has no regard for the inner life

Ralph remembered another small boy who had stood like this: he is recalling the boy who was killed in the bush fire

Percival Wemys Madison ...: the name and address are recognisably upper-middle class. This is clearly a well brought-up child, according to the standards of the world he has left behind, because he is able to recite his name and address efficiently and helpfully. But when rescue comes, the 'incantation had faded clean away' (p.222)

... maybe it's only us: Simon's intuition leads him to the heart of the fear which, in greater or lesser degree, afflicts all the boys. It is left to us, however, to decide whether Golding sees the evil in us as a theological condition (Original Sin), or as a natural disposition to destroy social order, or as a deep-rooted product of the imagination. The most satisfactory explanation is that it encompasses all three

Nuts!: Schoolboy slang for 'nonsense!'

the one crude expressive syllable: Jack thinks of the worst swear word he knows in order to ridicule Simon

The world, that understandable and lawful world, was slipping away: the majority of the boys have voted that they do believe in ghosts. Ralph sees the threat of irrational convictions replacing solid reason

Bollocks to the rules!: a vulgar and aggressive assertion of contempt for what Ralph is trying to enforce

Three blind mice: a phrase from a nursery rhyme, the earliest trace of which is in Ravenscroft's *Deuteromelia* (1609):

> Three blind mice, see how they run!
> They all ran after the farmer's wife,
> Who cut off their tails with a carving-knife,
> Did you ever see such a thing in your life
>   As three blind mice?

Ralph, Piggy and Simon feel equally helpless before Jack's self-assertion

Chapter 6 Beast from Air

All the children drift into a restless sleep. In the middle of the moonlit night the sign that Ralph had wanted descends upon the top of the hill— a dead airman killed in a far-off battle whose parachute has blown him towards the island and dropped him there to bow and sink in the wind.

Next morning the twins Sam and Eric have allowed the fire to go out, but they revive it and warm themselves. As they do so their eyes alight on the dead parachutist. In terror they rush back to the camp and wake Ralph, telling him they have seen the beast.

Ralph calls an assembly, not this time by blowing the conch (he perhaps thinks it would attract the beast) but through word of mouth. The twins tell their terrible story, their imaginations spinning fantasy from the reality they saw. Jack demands an immediate hunt for the beast, but Ralph points out their responsibilities to the littluns as well as the impracticality of tracking a creature that leaves no trail. He organises a proper hunt to the only part of the island to which Jack's hunters have never been.

The hunt for the beast begins, with Piggy left in charge of the littluns. Simon is included among the trackers, feeling bad that he has not the courage to tell his companions that the only kind of beast he can ever imagine is in human form.

Near the place they suspect the beast of inhabiting Ralph proves his chieftaincy by setting out for a solo reconnaissance but Jack follows him and soon the rest of the boys come too. To Ralph's exasperation, they are constantly diverted by exciting things to do like rolling rocks and he finds great difficulty in getting them to act responsibly about what they ought to be doing.

NOTES AND GLOSSARY:

other lights in the sky, that moved fast, winked, or went out ...: the aerial battle going on in the distant sky. The war that made it necessary to evacuate the boys and which was responsible for shooting down their plane is still, it seems, going on in the adult world beyond the island

So as the stars moved across the sky, the figure sat on the mountain-top and bowed and sank and bowed again: to the children the figure seems like a grotesque beast, but at this point Golding's language suggests to the adult reader something more like a god presiding over the island with ritual observance

Waxy: quick-tempered

Remember old Waxy at school? 'Boy-you-are-driving-me-slowly-insane!': the twins are recalling a schoolmaster nicknamed Waxy, and they imitate his style of speech

feeding the ponies over the garden wall: Ralph dreams of a pleasant, rural England

the 'beast': Sam and Eric describe the 'beast' so excitedly that they forget to distinguish what they really saw from what they imagine

Sucks to the littluns!: Jack's expression means 'what do the young children matter?' It indicates his lack of compassion, for he feels no responsibility towards people weaker than himself

For all we know, the beast may swing through the trees like what's its name: he means Tarzan or King Kong. These characters are well known in popular fiction and as the subject of a number of successful films. Tarzan lives like an ape, though he is an intelligent and athletic man. King Kong is a giant ape who is taken from a Pacific island to be exhibited in America

Soon, in a matter of centuries ... : Golding emphasises the vast time-scale of natural evolution. By implication the human adventure on the island has only an ephemeral significance

like the breathing of some stupendous creature: Golding re-creates Ralph's imagination which starts to see everything, even the sea, as a potential beast

the sleeping leviathan: here, the tide, derived from a biblical source referring to a huge whale, but subsequently meaning any monster of enormous size. ('There is that Leviathan, whom thou has made to play therein', Psalm 104:26)

guano: excrement of sea-birds. Since these droppings are particularly associated with islands off the coast of Peru we may have some justification for giving a slightly more specific location to the story

off your rockers: mad

Chapter 7 Shadows and Tall Trees

The tracking party rest and eat. Ralph contemplates the sea which seems different on this side of the island from the side where they are encamped. Simon seems to read his thoughts and assures him that he will get home eventually.

The hunt resumes with Jack suggesting that they should look for meat to kill at the same time as they seek the beast. Ralph's thoughts return to the comfortable England he has left behind. Suddenly a boar breaks cover and interrupts his reverie. Ralph is the first to take aim with his improvised spear and, though the animal escapes, he boasts afterwards of his quality as a hunter. The boys become excited by the talk of blood and make a circle around one of their number, Robert, whom they tease as though he were a cornered pig. Ralph joins in, as frenzied as the others by the instinct to destroy. Their 'game' comes to an end, though, before any real harm is done.

The day is drawing in again and the boys begin to have second thoughts about climbing the hill to find the beast. Ralph remembers their responsibilities to Piggy and the littluns, whom they have left behind, but feels the trackers can only spare one of their number to return and tell the others that the party will not be back till after dark. Simon volunteers.

More tension accumulates between Ralph and Jack about what to do next. Ralph advises postponing the hunt until tomorrow and has the support of the rest, though all believe it is tiredness, not fear, which makes them want to delay. Jack resents their decision and says he will go after the beast alone, implying that Ralph is a coward for not coming too. Ralph accepts the challenge and the two boys set out for the top of the hill. Almost at once Roger joins them. The boys bicker with each other as they move upwards, with Jack eventually going on alone.

Jack returns hurriedly to where Ralph and Roger are sitting nervously. He has seen the beast. Ralph decides that they should all go up and see what is there. Tentatively the three boys approach the beast. The dead parachutist continues to sit where he fell, his decomposing head occasionally rising in the wind. When the children see his face they flee down the hillside, stricken by the horror.

NOTES AND GLOSSARY:

Be sucking my thumb next: Ralph sees the temptation to regress, which the island seems to encourage

the spectacular dirt of boys who have fallen into mud or been brought down hard on a rainy day: more recollections of England, of boyish games which lead to falling into the mud or being tackled in a game of rugby football. Ralph dwells again on his English upbringing. Everything he recalls indicates a comfortable, middle-class existence. Chatham and Devonport are important naval bases in the south of England. 'Mummy', 'Daddy', 'wild ponies', 'that bright copper kettle and the plate with the little blue men', 'cornflakes with sugar and cream': all would be recalled by a child who has known only comfort and love

Boy's Book of Trains ...: typical books that an English middle-class boy would have in his bedroom

Berengaria: the Queen of Richard I of England. Legend has it that she ministered to her husband by sucking his battle wounds. She died c.1230

rugger: rugby football

Ralph looked at the sun critically. 'Early evening. After tea-time, at any rate.': Golding reminds us that some of the boys are still conditioned by the social norms of their lost world. Ralph talks as though the English social habit of afternoon tea at four o'clock was still being observed on the island

Windy: frightened

the ruin of a face: the dead parachutist is decomposing. Each time one of the boys sees him his flesh has deteriorated further. The same will be true of the pig's head, the Lord of the Flies

---

Chapter 8 Gift for the Darkness

Dawn is breaking. Ralph, Jack and Roger have returned to the camp and are telling Piggy what they saw. No one seems to know what to do next and there is renewed tension. Jack blows the conch, inexpertly, in order to summon an assembly. Ralph tries to assume command of the meeting but hands over to Jack, who makes a public denunciation of Ralph's moral claim to chieftaincy. He calls for a vote to reject Ralph, but no one raises a hand. Jack sobs with humiliation and runs away.

Simon now suggests to the meeting that they should return to the top of the hill, but no one is prepared to do this. Piggy suggests that they move the fire from the hill to the beach: it will be less effective as a signal to rescuers but out of range of the beast. The children gather wood and Piggy himself makes the flame. But once the fire is lit Ralph notices that some of the bigger children have wandered away, that, in fact, of the senior boys only Piggy, the twins and a few others remain with him.

Jack has gathered the deserters around him. He plans to kill a pig and leave out some of its meat to appease the beast. He and his hunters follow a pig-trail to find a large sow feeding her young. There ensues a hectic pursuit of the sow, culminating in her bloody and violent slaughter. The sow's head is placed on a stick and left in the woods as an offering for the beast.

Simon has wandered off from Ralph and Piggy not to become one of Jack's hunters but to his own secret place in the woods. He comes across the grinning head of the dead pig, 'the Lord of the Flies'.

Back on the beach Ralph and Piggy speculate about why things have gone wrong. They are interrupted by Jack and some of his hunters, all painted and naked. Some steal fire while Jack disdainfully invites Ralph and Piggy to share in the pig-meat that night. When he goes Ralph calls a meeting of the few remaining boys and littluns; he still tries to insist on sensible priorities but the attraction of eating meat exerts a strong pull over all of them, even Piggy.

Simon communes with the Lord of the Flies, who seems to tell him that he is both the beast and yet just a pig on a stick: that, in the end, he is part of Simon himself. Simon passes out—the heat? an epileptic fit?—with the Lord of the Flies continuing to mock his attempt to understand the situation in which the boys have found themselves on the island.

NOTES AND GLOSSARY:

'So we can't have a signal fire ... We're beaten.' A point of gold appeared above the sea and at once all the sky brightened.: Golding contrasts Ralph's despair at lacking a fire with the regularity of the sunrise. It is another example of how the natural world shows up human inadequacies

He isn't a proper chief: Jack publicly denounces Ralph. In allegorical terms this is an act of political rebellion and moral anarchy

I'm not going to play any longer: Jack's belligerence subsides, to be replaced by the tantrum of a child

cracked: mad

Each of them wore the remains of a black cap and ages ago they had stood in two demure rows and their voices had been the song of angels: the decline of the boys' moral state manifests itself visually. The tattered clothes and the singing voices that they use now only for hunting rites testify to their abandonment of order and restraint

He was happy and wore the damp darkness of the forest like his old clothes: of all the boys Jack most readily fits into the natural world, adapting to it physically and emotionally

the pigs lay ... sensuously enjoying the shadows under the trees ...: the paragraph portrays complete natural harmony, an Eden into which evil has not yet been introduced

This dreadful eruption from an unknown world: the boys have imported the blood-lust of another kind of life to a world which does not appear to have known it before. The island on which Golding sets *Lord of the Flies* enjoys an extraordinarily unviolated calm before the human intervention effectively disrupts it for ever

Then Jack grabbed Maurice and rubbed the stuff over his cheeks: a blooding ceremony, such as can be found both in primitive societies and in the sophisticated fox-hunting world of England. Jack is addressed as 'Chief' now

Sharpen a stick at both ends: to impale the sow's head

the Lord of the Flies: the first use of the phrase within the text of the novel. It is applied, of course, to the pig's head which Jack and his hunters have mounted on a stick, and which Simon now contemplates

that ancient, inescapable recognition: Golding deliberately leaves this phrase elliptical and enigmatic, for to spell out its intention too literally would take from the reader our own response to it. Simon appears to see in the Lord of the Flies the evidence for man's instinct towards evil. It is, in other words, a manifestation of the dark side of human nature and evidence of the human will to destroy. But Golding leaves room for us to interpret Simon's experience here according to our larger view of the whole novel

We just got to go on, that's all. That's what grown-ups would do: Piggy continues to refer to the adult world as the only standard of normality that he can conceive

taboo: prohibition. The word is normally used of primitive societies. Its use here crucially affects our understanding of the book, for we infer from it that Jack's name has started to acquire a mystique which previously only the conch shell possessed. A 'taboo' essentially concerns the banning or forbidding of something because some kind of fear has grown up around it. This is particularly appropriate of Jack's influence and had never been true when Ralph was in absolute command

demoniac: like demons; the word stresses the uncivilised pagan appearance of the hunters

He was safe from shame or self-consciousness behind the mask of his paint: much anthropological research has stressed the importance of mask, paint and other modes of disguise in any primitive community that hunts or goes to war. They confer dignity, terrify the victim or the enemy, and instil self-confidence

savages: Golding adopts an explicit vocabulary to demonstrate the regressive nature of Jack's band of hunters

You are a silly little boy ... : the Lord of the Flies does not actually speak, of course; Golding dramatises a dialogue that exists only in Simon's head

one of his times was coming on: the fit is possibly epileptic. Simon has passed out many times before

we shall do you: we shall kill you

Chapter 9 A View to a Death

A storm is building up. Simon has drifted from his fit into sleep. When he wakes he leaves the Lord of the Flies propped on the stick and wanders through the woods. He comes to the place where the dead parachutist sits. The rotting corpse sickens him but he realises that it is not a beast. He unloosens the parachute lines from where they have been caught in the rocks and decides that the other children must know the truth as soon as possible. He starts to stagger down the hill.

Ralph and Piggy have now been deserted by all but some littluns. They play games in the sea but are also tempted to join Jack's party. They find the feast is under way, presided over by the garlanded presence of Jack himself. They are given meat to eat, which they accept.

After the feast Jack is able to capitalise on his generosity to Ralph by interpreting it as the latter's renunciation of his right to be chief. Ralph protests ineffectively. At this point the storm breaks. The excited boys begin to dance in honour of their triumph as hunters. Chanting and movement combine to whip them into a frenzy. At the height of their celebration Simon emerges from the woods, and they all set upon him with sticks and hands while he cries about the dead man on the hill. No one listens, for, whipped up by their confusion of passion, blood-lust and terror of the beast, they tear Simon apart.

The storm lifts the parachutist from his resting-place on the island and carries him out to sea. Then the storm abates and a great calmness descends, during which Simon's body, beautiful in the moonlight, is also borne out to the open sea.

NOTES AND GLOSSARY:
The opening paragraph of this chapter again emphasises the huge scale of the natural world and the comparative puniness of the human. The 'build-up of clouds' and 'revolving masses of gas' are juxtaposed with the broken blood vessel in Simon's nose.

like an old man: the symbolic tone of this suggests that Simon's confrontation with the Lord of the Flies, and his consequent perception that evil lies within the heart of man himself, has not merely wearied him physically but made him the repository of all wisdom.

The confrontation with the dead parachutist com-
plements that with the Lord of the Flies. Both are
rotting. Simon's experience here completes his
knowledge of how humanity works and what the
nature of the evil is that afflicts the other boys

Keep your hair on: colloquial phrase for 'keep calm'

Jack ... sat there like an idol: Golding stresses the pagan element in what
Jack represents

Who'll join my tribe and have fun?: Jack's appeal to the pleasure-loving
side of his supporters contrasts with the responsi-
bility Ralph had displayed at earlier meetings. The
word 'tribe', like 'savages', has an anthropologically
exclusive sense, suggesting the self-sufficiency and
primitive pride of Jack's group

Do our dance! Come on! Dance!: Jack forestalls disruption of his
authority by releasing the pent-up energies of his
supporters. Ralph, by contrast, had always insisted
on rigid self-discipline

Simon was crying out something about a dead man on a hill: Simon tries to
tell the boys the truth about the beast, but they are
too excited to listen. The beauty of the sea, and the
power of the cosmos controlling its tidal movement,
converts the human horror of Simon's murder into
a scene of tranquillity and dignity

Chapter 10 The Shell and the Glasses

Ralph and Piggy have been abandoned by all but the twins and a few
littluns. They talk over what they and the other boys have done in killing
Simon. Ralph faces the situation more honestly than Piggy and the
twins, who would prefer not to talk about it. Jack has organised his
group with look-outs and imposed strong discipline. He commands
them to watch out for Ralph and Piggy and to beware of the beast.

Ralph and his remaining supporters are almost in despair. They try to
sleep, but as they start to dream their shelter is attacked by Jack's
marauders. In the ensuing scuffle Piggy's broken spectacles are stolen,
though the conch is left untouched.

NOTES AND GLOSSARY:

He may still be—: Piggy holds out hope that Simon may still be alive

Hullo. Fancy meeting you, Ralph ...: the conversation between Ralph,
Piggy and the twins on this page is full of the
ordinary niceties of social chit-chat, but the serious
issues remain known, though unsaid

the Castle Rock: the capital letters indicate how Jack has given names to the key places in his realm

Halt! Who goes there?: the traditional challenge of sentries on watch

He's going to beat Wilfred: this is the only mention Wilfred receives in the book, but his punishment (for an unstated reason) shows Jack's inclination to authoritarian, even tyrannous, rule

We might get taken prisoner by the reds: the Communists might capture us. This is the typical language of a child brought up in the cold-war atmosphere of Europe in the early 1950s

Wiltshire ... Devon: comfortable rural counties in the south of England. Dartmoor is, by English standards, very wild, remote and therefore romantic to a growing boy who knows he has a secure home to return to at the end of an adventurous day. To Ralph, isolated on a barbaric Pacific island, 'the attraction of wildness had gone'.

barmy; round the bend; bomb happy; crackers: all these are adjectives expressive of madness. 'Bomb happy' is Air Force slang from the Second World War and now sounds dated. The others are in regular schoolboy or colloquial usage

the pills: the testicles

Chapter 11 Castle Rock

Ralph, Piggy, Sam and Eric confer. Without Piggy's spectacles they cannot make a fire and they know that Jack will not use his fire as a signal to rescuers. Their position is hopeless. Piggy decides to go to Jack, believing that if he carries the conch with him Jack will find its authority irresistible. He will make an appeal to Jack's better nature to get his glasses back. Ralph and the twins agree to accompany him, Ralph insisting that they will not paint themselves when they appear before Jack.

Ralph leads the way to Jack's camp. He blows the conch to summon a new assembly. Jack confronts Ralph with an assertion that he now rules this end of the island. The two leaders quarrel and start fighting man-to-man. In a pause for breath Ralph tries to reason with Jack about why Piggy should have his spectacles back and how necessary it is to maintain the fire. Jack shows his sternness by ordering his 'guards' to grab hold of the twins Sam and Eric and tie them up.

Ralph and Jack resume their fight. Piggy tries to intervene, waving the conch ineffectively. He appeals for sense but his audience starts to stone him. Roger, higher than the rest, levers a large boulder which knocks Piggy over the cliff into the sea. He is killed instantly. The conch, too, has been smashed into fragments.

Ralph flees. Sam and Eric are left in the hands of Jack and Roger. Torture seems imminent.

NOTES AND GLOSSARY:

Give me my glasses, I'm going to say—you got to!: Piggy intends appealing to Jack's moral sense, ignorant of the fact that he rules without any

Behind them on the grass the headless and paunched body of a sow lay where they had dropped it: killing has now become routine to Jack and the hunters

You aren't playing the game—: Ralph uses a phrase derived from the good sportsmanship with which he has been inculcated in his English school. The giggles it elicits from 'the tribe' demonstrate how ineffective the old rules have become

Samneric protested out of the heart of civilization. 'Oh, I say!' '—honestly!': the twins use ludicrously polite expressions of protest. Golding wants to show the absurdity of good social manners in a situation where they are redundant. The destruction of the conch shell and Piggy's death coincide, representing the loss both of judicial and of intellectual reasoning among the boys

The hangman's horror clung round him: Roger has taken on the role of executioner. He levered the boulder which killed Piggy and now he advances on the twins with the power to torture

---

Chapter 12 Cry of the Hunters

Ralph has gone into hiding. His concern now is to survive and not to be caught by Jack, who, he knows, will never let him alone. He finds his way to the place where the Lord of the Flies is propped on a stick, but there is only a skull there 'that gleamed as white as ever the conch had done'. He strikes at the skull with his stick and splits it.

Night falls. Ralph feels isolated and bitter. In the distance he can hear Jack's crowd celebrating. He comes close to Sam and Eric, who are terrified at his sudden appearance. He persuades them to talk, though they are now in Jack's service. They hint at the strategy which will be used to hunt and possibly kill Ralph the next day. But they give Ralph some meat to eat before he leaves them.

He finds his way into a secluded thicket much closer to Jack's camp than he thinks they will suspect. He sleeps. In the morning he hears Jack talking to the twins and learns that the general area of his hiding-place is known. After some while Jack's people heave boulders onto his shelter but Ralph is not hurt. A sharpened stick probes the thicket, but Ralph injures the bearer. Then he realises that he is being smoked out. The undergrowth has been set alight.

Ralph is flushed into the open. He injures another 'savage'. He tries hard to think rationally about the best means of self-defence. He careers aimlessly through the woods, coming back to the place where the pig's skull lies broken. He takes refuge in another thicket, but is again discovered by Jack's searchers. He rushes from the woods, with the howling mob in pursuit some way behind.

Ralph emerges on to the open beach, falling over and 'trying to cry for mercy'. He finds himself facing a British naval officer, immaculately uniformed and speaking English. Jack's party emerges from the woods, no longer in murderous pursuit of Ralph but standing in a meek semicircle while the officer asks his questions. The grown-up views the children a little critically, as though they have let down the best standards of their upbringing, but he accepts that for them everything must be just fun and games.

Ralph sobs and soon the other boys weep too. The naval officer prepares to take them off the island.

NOTES AND GLOSSARY:

Then there was that indefinable connection between himself and Jack: Golding touches on an archetypal theme, the mutual attraction of enemies. Compare Caius Martius and Tullus Aufidius in Shakespeare's *Coriolanus* or Wilfred Owen's poem 'Strange Meeting' ('I am the enemy you killed, my friend')

the skull that gleamed as white as ever the conch had done: the pig's head (Lord of the Flies) and the conch shell are now equated, the representation of evil and the symbol of it, so that both evil and good have been expunged from the island: in symbolic terms no moral poles now survive

Roger sharpened a stick at both ends: clearly a reminder of the first pig slaughter (see Chapter 8, Jack's instruction to Roger, 'Sharpen a stick at both ends'). The twins imply that if Ralph is caught, his head will be impaled upon the stick. He will be the new Lord of the Flies

ululating: howling

diddle: cheat

pax: (*Latin:* peace) schoolboy slang for 'truce'

a deep grumbling noise ... He knew he had heard it before, but had no time to remember: only at the end of the book can we put this noise into context. Ralph hears the noise of a boat's engine as it comes to the shore

a sound ... too low to hear: the boat again

... trying to cry for mercy: Ralph, in his terror and in a situation where the language of his former existence is meaningless, cannot find any words to express his appeal for life

The officer nodded, as if a question had been answered: he recognises that the child before him can speak English

Part 3

Commentary

General points

William Golding has described *Lord of the Flies* as a fable. In saying this he points to the simplicity with which the story is told. A fable normally illustrates a fundamental aspect of human behaviour which might otherwise be explained only in a work of great complexity. Because the form of the story is clearly set out, with few diversions of sub-plot and with fairly obvious contrasts of character, it may be that some readers will approach the novel merely as an adventure story. To some extent they are right to do so. A great deal of serious criticism discusses *Lord of the Flies* only in terms of its philosophical implications and forgets that Golding has written an exciting tale to which readers of most ages can respond. He has retold *The Coral Island* (see Plot and structure, pp. 43–4) in an atmosphere of menace, matching a mid-twentieth-century mood as surely as R.M. Ballantyne did the mid-nineteenth century.

The novel's profundities cannot be overlooked, however, and in the sections following we examine its philosophical substance—remembering that philosophy touches not just upon metaphysics but upon politics, anthropology, morality and theology. There follows consideration of the novel as allegory, and sections on plot and structure, language and imagery, and characterisation.

Given its intention to be a fable, and if we allow a writer to present his view of the human condition even if we do not share that view ourselves, *Lord of the Flies* is undoubtedly well told and subtly argued. If it has weaknesses, they are of three kinds and all of them may be disputed.

First, the novel has a slight tendency to glibness: that is, the allegorical pattern necessitates a streamlining of plot and character which sometimes seems to over-simplify its complex thesis.

Secondly, the novel has dated a little since it was published in 1954. Occasionally this is a matter of language—English schoolboys no longer say 'Wacco!' and a later writer would not be coy about 'the one crude expressive syllable' (Chapter 5)—but it may be in the subject too. Golding was responding to a particular kind of post-war pessimism, which he shared with writers like Albert Camus, Jean-Paul Sartre and Samuel Beckett. Though there is nothing in his later work to suggest that he himself has changed his mind about human nature it is undoubtedly true that more qualified and possibly optimistic views have been expressed by some of the major novelists of recent years.

Thirdly, Golding slightly inhibits his exploration of human behaviour by restricting his subject to a group of schoolboys. Their youth does not tell against them—it is part of the novel's theme that children have not yet been moulded into the settled prejudices of the adult world. But the fact that they are all male results in a total absence of the sexual part of human behaviour. Apart from the mutual fascination of Ralph and Jack, which is the admiration of heroes for each other, there is no hint of homosexuality in the novel and obviously no opportunity for heterosexuality either. Any attempt to allegorise human nature without paying due attention to our sexual responses must appear to be incomplete.

Lord of the Flies has set critics, students and ordinary readers discussing its theories with great earnestness, but there has been a tendency to depart from the novel as a work of literature in order to speculate on the ideas it suggests. These are obviously significant, as we see in the next section, but we must keep in mind that Golding presents us with an *imaginative* achievement first and foremost.

The philosophy of the novel

Many people who read *Lord of the Flies* have been known to comment, 'That's the book I would have written if only I'd got down to it.' Golding touched a nerve-end which any educated person will recognise in himself. We all acknowledge our schooldays as one of the formative periods of our lives, when 'civilisation' implants itself within us. What, Golding asks, would happen if the thin layers of knowledge, manners and culture which we acquire from our schoolteachers were to be peeled away? Is natural man, as opposed to cultivated man, a savage, a philistine and a marauder? These problems have, in one form or another, been posed in most periods of intellectual history. Golding's achievement is not to have initiated discussion of man's basic nature but to have found a form for talking about these issues in a thoroughly contemporary manner.

We have seen in Part 1 that the disillusioned post-war atmosphere of the 1950s, when atomic catastrophe seemed to face man more obviously than perhaps it does today, greatly colours the mood of *Lord of the Flies*. Only a few years later the philosopher Bertrand Russell was to write a book entitled *Has Man A Future?*—the title clearly raised doubts about the survival of the human race. Golding's contribution to the pessimism which characterises so much of the important writing of the mid-twentieth century was to probe the inner recesses of human behaviour to see by what instincts we are governed. His way of doing this was to create a fiction in which a group of children, not yet completely conditioned by the adult world, would be stranded on a desert island and left to fend for themselves. The thesis lying behind Golding's story presumes that in such a situation man reverts to his natural self. His hunger, his fear and his selfishness assert themselves at the expense of his compassion and his rationality. These latter qualities can flourish only in the protected conditions of 'civilised' society.

The conflict between our civilised selves and our brutal inner nature comprises one of the archetypal clashes of literature: Cain and Abel in the Book of Genesis, Prospero and Caliban in Shakespeare's *The Tempest*, the Houyhnhnms and the Yahoos in Swift's *Gulliver's Travels*. Golding weights the scales against man's civilised side by making the failures of the adult world in *Lord of the Flies* explicit and total. The children in the novel are partly the victims of adult self-destruction. We do not know why a war rages in the background of the book, responsible for the children's being on the island after their aeroplane has been shot down and for the existence of the dead parachutist on the hill. Golding's interest lies less in causes than in consequences. All we know is that the northern hemisphere has become unsafe for children of the next generation. They have been evacuated to Gibraltar, then to Addis Ababa, and have now crash-landed while flying over a Pacific atoll, moving at each stage further south from their own society. That area of the world which most prides itself on its culture and science has become uninhabitable for its young people.

In reading *Lord of the Flies* we should not forget the world still fighting beyond the island on which the story is set. Though the parachutist demonstrably reminds us of this other world, Golding constantly has the children referring to it in contrast to their present existence. Ironically they tend to miss its comforts—ponies, warm hearths, games of football—and have scant conception of its horrors. The reader, though, is not allowed to forget them: even at the end of the novel the uniformed naval officer and the ratings with their sub-machine guns remind us of the brutal world elsewhere. By creating a 'civilisation' where devastation seems to prevail over creativeness, Golding significantly directs our responses to the boys' degeneration in the novel. They do not only revert to a basic barbarism which Golding suggests may lie under the veneer of education and culture. They grow up into small adults emulating the 'real' world they have left behind and to which eventually they return. It seriously over-simplifies the novel to see it merely as charting a regression in the boys. Golding is also concerned with the hideous nature of their growing up.

Lord of the Flies proposes a view of man's essential nature which one might more normally expect to find argued in a philosophical treatise or in a theological work. Indeed, if the reader feels sometimes that the plotting of this novel is too schematic and relentless, this may be because

Golding is more concerned to demonstrate his theory about the incipient self-centredness of the human species than to explore the psychology of individual characters. Everything has to conform to the pattern of behaviour he perceives as natural to man and which he therefore imposes upon the novel. We quickly sense the inevitability of the children's movement towards savagery, though Golding relates the story with such economy and intensity that its predictability does not become monotonous.

The clearest model for his thesis is Thomas Hobbes's *The Leviathan* (1651). Indeed, if the student of *Lord of the Flies* wants to read just one book as background to the novel then *The Leviathan* is a good choice. Hobbes (1588–1679) was an immensely influential political theorist whose notions about humanity had practical consequences for the founding of English democracy, as well as for the reassessment of man's view of himself in the decades during which the self-confidence of the European Renaissance began to wane. In *The Leviathan* Hobbes asserted that man is intrinsically selfish. He denied that man is by nature a social being (as the Greek philosopher Aristotle had maintained) and upheld instead that each individual is fundamentally guided by self-interest. As Hobbes puts it, 'I put for a generall inclination of all mankind, a perpetuall and restlesse desire of Power after power, that ceaseth only in Death' (*The Leviathan*, Part I, Chapter XI). To counter the anarchy which man's selfishness would create if there were no checks and balances to restrain it, we adopt, according to Hobbes, certain 'articles of peace' which impose restrictions on individual liberty. To see that these articles are implemented, an external power is entrusted with absolute authority, including the right to punish.

This power, in *Lord of the Flies*, is initially entrusted to Ralph by the common consent of the other children. When, however, he proves too ineffective as a leader (or, in Hobbesian language, a 'sovereign') he is displaced by the more ruthless figure of Jack. Hobbes suggests that the people's loyalty to the sovereign need only last as long as his authority effectively protects them. If his authority fails then they have the right to replace him by someone more competent—there is not, in other words, any supernatural or extra-social factor (like the Divine Right claimed by medieval kings) that the leader can cite as justification for his rule. Hobbes denies that any man possesses an instinct to do good or to feel loyalty or to defend his friend. When these things occur it can only be as an act of self-interest. The leader, if he should fail the people in any way, cannot presume on the support or love of anyone. The multitude, he says, 'will clamour, fight against, and destroy those, by whom all their life-time before, they have been protected, and secured from injury. And if this be Madnesse in the multitude, it is the same in every particular man' (*The Leviathan*, Part I, Chapter VIII).

Hobbes is not the only source for Golding's theory of human nature but *The Leviathan* provides a valid parallel with *Lord of the Flies*. Hobbes not only outlines how societies are formed but advances a psychological argument about our instinctive insecurity. The covenant man forms with his sovereign only exists because he fears the alternative lack of protection against the wildness of nature and the anarchistic opposition of his fellow-men. We see all this embodied in Golding's novel. The boys assemble on the beach in Chapter 1 in order to see what can be done *as a group*. It never occurs to any of them to act as a solitary individual, unencumbered by social responsibilities. Only Simon occasionally breaks away from the group to go off on his own, but when he does so he tries to think out what has happened not just to himself but to all his companions. His social sense never lapses.

The boys acknowledge Ralph as their leader because he happens to be in possession of the conch. Thereafter no one can expect to make a speech before the assembled children unless he has custody of the conch. Golding shows, by this means, how dependent we are in any organisation upon symbolic sanctions. It may be a crown, or a mace (such as must be present in the British House of Commons if the proceedings are to be valid), or a stool (in Ashanti society), or a holy book, or a special drink: whatever it is, no community can exist without symbol and ritual.

Jack's lack of expertise in blowing the conch and his growing neglect of the symbolic authority with which it has been invested clearly point to his abuse of social custom. By the end of the novel Jack is well on his way to establishing a tyranny. He has been able—according to the Hobbesian notion that no sovereign can depend upon the loyalty of his people if he has ceased to protect them—to subvert the other children, to win them away from Ralph, and to establish a system of 'government' depending on the strict maintenance of his tyrannical 'justice'. He metes out summary justice to any opponent—Piggy dies, Ralph is hounded, Wilfred is beaten, Samneric possibly tortured. He wields his authority by pandering to the fear of his subjects and offering them outlets for their apprehension. Under his rule the children have festivals and rites of a kind which Ralph can see only as a distraction from what ought to be everyone's principal objective: rescue.

More is at stake in the opposition of Ralph and Jack than two alternative forms of 'government'. In *Lord of the Flies* Golding concerns himself with moral issues as well as with political and social theory. Some critics have seen the boys' propensity to evil as evidence of Original Sin. This Christian doctrine presumes that since the Fall of Man (allegorised in the Book of Genesis as the story of Adam in Eden) we are all born into the world with inherited wickedness, from which we can be saved only by the loving forgiveness and grace of God. Certainly the island on which *Lord of the Flies* takes place enjoys an extraordinary natural bliss before the intervention of the boys. Golding presents several images of this harmony—the exquisite colouring of the conch as it lies quietly in the sea, the butterflies in Simon's retreat, the sow nurturing its young. The arrival of human beings invariably disturbs nature: from the scar left on the landscape by the crashed aeroplane to the raging fire which devastates the island at the end of the book, Golding presents many examples of man's rapacity. We may legitimately debate, however, whether these episodes point to Original Sin—which is a theological concept—or just to the incompatibility of human society with the natural world.

The novel acknowledges the religious needs of man. No character remains unaffected by the fear of the unknown which descends with the night. By daylight there are social duties to be performed, meals to be sought and cooked, shelters to be built, watch to be kept, but at night all kinds of inexplicable and irrational obsessions take hold of the boys. Many of them have nightmares. One of them, the boy with the mulberry birthmark, seems to go berserk. Fantasy replaces common sense. In this mood it is not difficult for supernatural beliefs to take root among the children. The decomposing parachutist on the hill—whose *real* existence reminds us of the sordidness of the *human* world—is easily converted into the beast-figure to which their lively imaginations have already given birth. The children create their own god. Under Jack's rule they start to worship it and to appease it. They place a sow's head on a stick and offer it as food for the beast. We are at the point in human evolution where man turns to idol-worship and ceremony as a means of allaying his terror of forces which he cannot intellectually understand. Through communal religious rites he can also consolidate his social unity and find a release for some of his neuroses. Only Simon comes to understand all this, but he is torn to pieces by the other boys before he can explain: passion destroys reason.

Though the children in *Lord of the Flies* create their own gods we need to be wary of dismissing religion from Golding's view of the universe. Like the English novelist, Thomas Hardy, whose novels have probably influenced him, Golding frequently reminds us of the immensity of the cosmos in relation to the puniness of man. *Lord of the Flies* abounds in sentences like 'Soon, in a matter of centuries, the sea would make an island of the castle' (Chapter 6), in which the scale of natural history is emphasised. Human achievements and failures seem unimportant by contrast to the regularity and impersonality of the universal process.

> Somewhere over the darkened curve of the world the sun and moon were pulling; and the film of water on the earth planet was held, bulging slightly on one side while the solid core turned. (Chapter 9)

Behind such order there may well exist a creative being, but Golding's characters do not speculate much on such a possibility:

> ... they grew accustomed to these mysteries and ignored them, just as they ignored the miraculous, throbbing stars. (Chapter 4)

They yield, instead, to domination by their own irrational fears. The only people who try to find explanations for what is happening to the boys—Simon, Ralph and Piggy—are either murdered or outlawed.

Simon, Ralph and Piggy serve as reminders in the novel that man's history has not been wholly black. Each of them displays positive qualities of vision or inventiveness. Simon is the most 'spiritual' character here, with a natural goodness that partly corrects the thesis of the rest of the novel. Though Simon dies at the hands of the other boys, Golding's portrayal of him cannot be easily eradicated from the reader's mind. In conception he owes something to Myshkin in Dostoievski's *The Idiot* (a fellow epileptic) or to the lunatic Benjy in William Faulkner's *The Sound and the Fury*: their mental frailty cloaks an intensity of perception. The other boys like to call him 'barmy' but for us he has the clearest view of all. Ralph is the planner whose main concern is to find a means of rescue, but who understands the need for self-discipline that this entails. Piggy is the inventor.

If the evil side of humanity leaves the stronger impression upon us when we have read *Lord of the Flies* we should perhaps reflect about how much the boys manage to achieve before they finally give way to fear and frenzy. They discover fire, they make shelters, they organise hunting expeditions, they explore the terrain, they allot social responsibilities. Nor does Jack's assumption of the leadership altogether discredit their inventiveness. He, after all, knows that survival is as important as rescue. Food has to be hunted; emotional needs (which Ralph tries to deny) have to be satisfied.

In the next section (Allegory and realism) and in the last section (The characters) of this part of the notes we see in more detail the significant role played in the allegorical scheme of the novel by individual characters. Ralph, for example, embodies some of the qualities of a king or chief, Jack is the usurper, Piggy both a chief adviser and the scientific brain, Roger the executioner, and Simon the prophet without honour in his own country. We need to beware of interpreting the novel only as a philosophical allegory, though it would be equally mistaken to underestimate the political and social theory or the moral analysis with which it deals. *Lord of the Flies* may be about man's preference for pleasure over duty, about his psychological needs, and about the way societies conduct themselves. It is also, however, about children. Golding might have established his themes by observing adult or even (as George Orwell (1903–50) does in *Animal Farm*) bestial behaviour. He chooses children because of their special vulnerability. In reading *Lord of the Flies* we do the book an injustice if we treat the boys merely as ciphers in an intellectual discussion. They always behave like real children who have suddenly become parentless. They start by facing the new experience as an adventure. This romantic attitude soon collapses, however, as physical needs and inner terrors assert themselves. If we are tempted to read *Lord of the Flies* purely as a theoretical treatise on human nature we may end up by making cerebral and academic one of the most acute studies of child psychology in modern English fiction.

Allegory and realism

All allegory is a form of extended metaphor. It must, therefore, need interpretation by the reader. The writer tells a tale behind which exists an explicit moral point. The narrative method is figurative: that is, characters, incidents and images stand for something else in the 'real' world. For this reason the details of an allegory must cohere firmly and it will often appear to be more schematic than actual life. An element of artificiality can be detected in most allegories.

Lord of the Flies contains allegorical elements. In the last section we have seen how these can be interpreted philosophically. We must bear the notion of allegory in mind as we read the novel in order to question each detail as we come to it by asking how everything fits into the allegorical structure. Sometimes the allegory imposes demands upon the structure and plotting of the story which might be unacceptable if the intention was purely realistic. For instance, the arrival on the hill of the dead parachutist and, even more, his departure from it after Simon's murder—these episodes are most improbable if we are reading *Lord of the Flies* as though it could really happen. They work figuratively. The parachutist represents the intrusion of the outside world at a time when Ralph has appealed for some such sign. The children do not see his rotting corpse for what it is but instead convert him into a devil or a beast. Whipped up by terror of their own fantasy they destroy the beast when they have the opportunity: in fact what they do is kill Simon, whom they confuse with the beast of the hill. The wind wafts the parachutist away from the hill to an unknown burial in the sea while the tide carries away Simon's body to a similar grave. These do not seem probable incidents if we are reading the novel only to see how a group of children cope with being stranded on a desert island. The moment, however, we recognise that Golding proposes a point of view about human nature we can see how necessary such incidents are to the scheme of the allegory. They have a poetic credibility. Though *Lord of the Flies* can be interpreted allegorically, the novel never loses touch with its contemporary society. Some allegories are so artificial that they become virtual fantasies: examples would include Orwell's *Animal Farm*, in which the animals' behaviour stands for the conduct of politicians, or Edmund Spenser's (1552?–99) *The Faerie Queene*, where figures from pageant and romance represent moral qualities as well as certain people of Spenser's own day. *Lord of the Flies* cannot be seen as allegory of this sort, for despite the improbability that life on the island might happen exactly as Golding presents it, nothing in the boys' behaviour strikes us as psychologically unconvincing. Whatever role each character has in the allegorical format of the novel each one acts naturalistically too.

Golding describes the landscape of the novel in great detail. Thus after a close reading it would be possible to draw a map of the island. This realistic accuracy is essential, for we must have a sense of how the 'mountain' dominates the interior, of the 'jungle' against which the boys have a constant physical struggle, of the cliff over which Piggy topples to his death, and of the separate ends of the island which effectively divide Jack's community from Ralph's.

Lest the setting of *Lord of the Flies* appear too exotic or unfamiliar to the reader Golding has the boys referring constantly to the world they have left behind. This is psychologically probable, but it also helps to bridge the gap between allegory and reality. This unnamed island in the Pacific Ocean, full of wild pigs and lush vegetation, should seem remote from us—the children must appear totally lost from western civilisation—but by counterpointing the foreignness of this setting with the known world of art, leisure, close-knit families and enough to eat (even if, in the terms of the novel, this world has been eliminated), Golding successfully underlines the children's tragedy.

Plot and structure

This section need not detain us for long since the essence of a well-told fable must be brevity and simplicity. Golding never wanders from his main themes, as outlined earlier in Part 3. There are no sub-plots or comic diversions. Even Simon's musings or Maurice's antics, which may not at first sight seem central to the story, all illustrate other facets of human nature.

The basis for *Lord of the Flies* is a novel first published in 1858 entitled *The Coral Island*. This book, by the Scottish author Robert Michael Ballantyne, has always been a great favourite with British school-children and has become one of the classic adventure tales written in English. Golding mentions it twice in the text, in Chapter 2, when one of the boys compares their situation with Ballantyne's story, and again on the last page, when the naval officer believes he has the measure of what has happened to the children by saying 'Jolly good show. Like the Coral Island.' In fact, life for Golding's children has been nothing like that enjoyed by Ballantyne's; the Scots novelist merely wanted to write a good adventure yarn. Golding, though, wanted to use *The Coral Island* as a model for *Lord of the Flies*, making his own novel an ironic commentary on its predecessor. The student of *Lord of the Flies* does not need to read Ballantyne, but it should interest him to know that there are many parallel incidents and characters in the two books. This even extends to the naming of the two central characters: Ralph and Jack are the names of Ballantyne's principals too. Piggy has his counterpart in a lad called Peterkin. Ballantyne's story hardly touches on the philosophical depths of Golding's (though it is not absolutely devoid of them), nor does it have the brutality of *Lord of the Flies*. Ballantyne, disguising himself as the hero Ralph Rover, says in the Preface to *The Coral Island* that he wants his readers to 'enter with kindly sympathy into the regions of fun'. This innocent statement aptly summarises his own achievement, but in the light of Golding's use of the word 'fun', to signify the breakdown of order, it takes on a new edge.

Golding does not allow cross-reference to Ballantyne to become an imprisoning device. He invents his own circumstances and renders them in a much more tightly knit form than Ballantyne does in his book. *Lord of the Flies* moves rapidly from event to event. The boys assemble, they organise themselves, they adjust to the island, they start disputes, they turn against each other, they destroy. The plot is very simple, remarkable for its relentless progression. The two incidents involving the outside world—the arrival of the dead parachutist and the appearance of the naval officer—are highly contrived, emphasising that we are reading fiction. The structure of the novel is similarly controlled, without ramblings of any kind. As it proceeds, the novel concentrates more and more on the rivalry of Ralph and Jack.

Language and imagery

The language of *Lord of the Flies* is generally extremely plain and functional. Golding does not attempt any passages of ornamental language, though occasionally he conveys a feeling of cosmic grandeur by using an elevated vocabulary. An example comes at the end of Chapter 9 when Simon's body is carried out to sea:

> Along the shoreward edge of the shallows the advancing clearness was full of strange, moonbeam-bodied creatures with fiery eyes. Here and there a larger pebble clung to its own air and was covered with a coat of pearls. The tide swelled in over the rain-pitted sand and smoothed everything with a layer of silver. Now it touched the first of the stains that seeped from the broken body and the creatures made a moving patch of light as they gathered at the edge. The water rose further and dressed Simon's coarse hair with brightness. The line of his cheek silvered and the turn of his shoulder became sculptured marble. The

strange, attendant creatures, with their fiery eyes and trailing vapours, busied themselves round his head.

On a literal level the passage describes the advancing tide as it starts to cover Simon's corpse, but Golding imagines the scene poetically. The 'moonbeam-bodied creatures with fiery eyes' are the shimmering stirrings of the sea as the moon shines upon it. A veil of bright whiteness covers everything, suggested by 'moonbeam', 'pearl', 'silver' and 'marble'. White being, in European culture, the traditional colour for innocence, we can see how the prose offers more than straightforward narrative description: it implies purification of the saintly Simon.

Golding's prose does not work as symbolically as this all the time. Indeed, the author places such poetic moments so selectively in the novel that they seem like oases of calm in the generally swift-moving narrative. The vocabulary in this novel is uncomplicated, the sentence structure avoids unnecessary elaborations, and the dialogue is terse and colloquial. As a writer of modern English prose Golding demonstrates excellently how complex philosophical and moral themes can be handled in unaffected language. The physical details of the novel are presented explicitly. Let us examine one example:

> Grass was worn away in front of each trunk but grew tall and untrodden in the centre of the triangle. Then, at the apex, the grass was thick again because no one sat there. All round the place of assembly the grey trunks rose, straight or leaning, and supported the low roof of leaves. On two sides was the beach; behind, the lagoon; in front, the darkness of the island. (Chapter 5)

This passage describes the boys' assembly area. The language never obtrudes between the reader and his imagined observation of the place, yet it presents the scene with astonishing accuracy. Not only do we have a clear idea of where it is in relation to other landmarks like the beach but we can see the worn patches of grass where the boys are likely to sit.

In choosing to write exclusively about children, Golding sets himself a problem from the outset. If he perceives the child's world entirely through an adult vocabulary then he runs the risk of removing that world too far from reality. Many an autobiography has failed because the venerable author looks back at his growing up from too lofty a height. Golding avoids the easy alternative (adopted, among others, by Ballantyne in *The Coral Island*) of putting the story into the first person and pretending that the tale is being told by one of the survivors of the experiences it recounts. Such a technique must lead to the development of a special relationship between narrator and reader which Golding wants to avoid. He wants us to see every character with equal dispassion. His solution avoids any kind of commitment to one character over the others and also avoids being patronising.

Golding uses a straightforward English that will be as intelligible to an educated adolescent as to a sophisticated adult. He incorporates within it, however, many indications of how children perceive their world. A community composed only of children, such as that in *Lord of the Flies*, will naturally use only the language of its own age group. Hence the schoolboy slang (instances of which are given in the notes to individual chapters in Part 2), the nicknames, the childish phrases like 'buzzed off' or Jack's 'I'm not going to play any longer. Not with you' (Chapter 8). To the child's perspective the hill looks like a mountain, so Golding calls it 'the mountain' throughout the novel. The sticks they use as weapons become 'spears'. He shows the boys giggling over the daring use of a word which would not be permitted in the adult world. Without condescending to his characters he enters their perspective on life by means of his well-judged language.

The novel does not stress the class distinctions between the boys, but some suggestion that Piggy comes from a less privileged background than the others emerges not just from what he tells us about his life but from the kind of language he uses. He speaks less grammatically than the others, with a distinct Cockney intonation: 'And this is what the tube done'; 'I don't like them clouds.'

Golding has the ability, when appropriate, to match the rhythm of his prose with the subject matter. We see an example in Chapter 1, when the boys are diverted by the fun of rock-rolling (an incident which takes on a different tone when we read later in the novel of Piggy's being deliberately toppled to his death by a rock):

The rock was as large as a small motor car.
'Heave!'
Sway back and forth, catch the rhythm.
'Heave!'
Increase the swing of the pendulum, increase, increase, come up and bear against that point of furthest balance—increase—increase—
'Heave!'
The great rock loitered, poised on one toe, decided not to return, moved through the air, fell, struck, turned over, leapt droning through the air and smashed a deep hole in the canopy of the forest.

The movement of the prose suggests the swaying of the rock before it crashes down; the repeated word 'increase' helps the tension to mount; and the short staccato words 'fell, struck, turned over, leapt . . . smashed' capture the bumps as the object falls to the ground.

Golding's imagery in *Lord of the Flies* is conventional, although he renders it with freshness. He highlights the malevolence of what the boys do on the island by contrasting the human disruptions with the harmony and peace of nature. If we examine the scene before the first pig-slaughter we can see how the boys transform a natural idyll into something monstrous:

> The pigs lay, bloated bags of fat, sensuously enjoying the shadows under the trees. There was no wind and they were unsuspicious ... Under the trees an ear flapped idly. A little apart from the rest, sunk in deep maternal bliss, lay the largest sow of the lot. She was black and pink; and the great bladder of her belly was fringed with a row of piglets that slept or burrowed and squeaked. (Chapter 8)

There could not be a clearer image of natural bliss, with the word 'unsuspicious' emphasising the Eden-like innocence of the scene. Yet Jack selects this sow for his victim, tracks it, kills it, offers its head to the gods, so that in time it becomes metamorphosed into the Lord of the Flies of the novel's title.

Much of the imagery in the story derives from this contrast between nature and man. Certain key words like 'devil' often recur in order to emphasise the evil atmosphere which descends upon the island. In the end, however, both language and imagery serve the archetypal elements of the novel. Large general phrases lie embedded amid the explicit physical detail and natural symbolism already noticed:

> If faces were different when lit from above or below—what was a face? What was anything? (Chapter 5)

or Simon's communion with the Lord of the Flies:

> 'I'm part of you? Close, close, close! I'm the reason why it's no go. Why things are what they are?' (Chapter 8)

or, perhaps most moving of all, the final glimpse we have of Ralph, weeping:

> for the end of innocence, the darkness of man's heart, and the fall through the air of the true, wise friend called Piggy, (Chapter 12)

Golding's achievement in *Lord of the Flies* is as much linguistic as philosophical, for he successfully marries these metaphysical abstractions with a convincingly evoked child's world. The language unites symbol and reality in as effective a way as in any modern English novel.

The characters

Ralph

We encounter Ralph on the first page of the novel. He is twelve years old, athletically built, good-looking and from a prosperous, middle-class family. He has natural qualities of leadership which do not depend merely upon his possession of the conch, but these qualities do not include the ruthlessness and assertiveness needed to counter Jack's opposition. Ralph thinks slowly, step by step, and is usually dependent upon Piggy's inspiration. He is the only boy to set his mind on the ultimate necessity of rescue. Despite some weakness in his character, Ralph has a natural disposition to be kind and to do good. He feels responsibility for the littluns and guilt over his participation in Simon's death. Ralph's moral sense survives longer than any other character. At the end of the book, when he has been hounded to exhaustion and believes himself likely to be executed, we find this moral instinct still preserved: 'he was down ... trying to cry for mercy'. The origins of his trust in moral principles can be seen at the beginning: 'there was a mildness about his mouth and eyes that proclaimed no devil'. Perhaps Ralph's most notable quality is his conscience, which leads him to puzzle and worry over the welfare of the other boys.

Jack

Jack Merridew enters the novel at the head of a procession of choirboys which appears as 'something dark ... the creature'. He is wearing a swirling black cloak, part of his ecclesiastical uniform. Thereafter he is always associated with shadows, and lack of light. He contrasts physically with the fair-haired Ralph, being 'ugly without silliness'. He differs too from Ralph in his lack of sympathy for the other boys. He lays claim to be chief early on, on the irrelevant grounds that he is head boy of his school and can sing C sharp. He never accepts defeat gracefully and sets himself in competition with Ralph from the start, eventually taking over the leadership because he can promise more 'fun' than his rival. There are occasions when he can seem quite vulnerable, as when he finds himself incapable of slaughtering a pig, but generally he tends towards physical toughness, lack of moral scruples and a love of the exercise of power. However, he understands better than Ralph that the children's fears cannot be dismissed. He learns to exploit these, partly because he shares them. He represents more completely than anyone else in the novel the theme of 'reversion to savagery'. He finds that behind the disguise of paint and mask he can assume a more self-confident personality.

Piggy

Piggy joins Ralph on the first page of the novel. From the start it is clear from his bad grammar—'I can't hardly move with all these creeper things'—that he has a less polished education than the other boys in the story. He is an unprepossessing youth, fat and greedy, as his nickname implies. We never learn his real name. He suffers from ill health and short-sightedness, and tends to fuss about both. He often seems old before his time, referring to the other children as 'a crowd of kids', yet he greatly fears being left alone. He is the most intellectual of the children on the island, the only one for whom the absence of books must be a real deprivation. Often he sounds a cold voice of common sense which the others may not like to hear ('they don't know where we are 'cos we never got there', he says in Chapter 2, speaking of the adult world). Though he lacks the ability of Ralph or Jack to impress an audience he sometimes hits on the most sensible suggestions for what to do next. Ralph, towards whom, after an initial cautiousness, Piggy maintains real loyalty, comes to value his wisdom and decency. In an allegorical interpretation of the novel Piggy represents man's capacity to invent; his death shows the intolerance of society towards its thinkers. 'Life is scientific', says Piggy, but his tragedy is that few of the boys are prepared to agree.

Simon

William Golding has described Simon as 'a Christ-figure ... a lover of mankind, a visionary' (*The Hot Gates*, pp.97–8). We first meet him anonymously: he is the fainting child of whom Jack speaks disparagingly in Chapter 1. Thereafter we see more of him alone than in company, for his shyness makes it difficult for him to summon up the courage to speak publicly. Yet his affection for the other boys never wanes. He dies trying to give them the simple enlightenment that the beast they fear is only a rotting corpse. Simon makes the intuitive discovery that all the terrors on the island exist within the boys themselves. His confrontation with the Lord of the Flies brings on an epileptic fit but in the crisis preceding it he manages to mouth the words 'Pig's head on a stick', his recognition that nothing evil exists in nature other than what man invests with his own evil. Simon's death at the hands of his own companions, to whom he tries to reveal a fundamental truth, gives him some of the attributes of a martyr.

Roger

This malevolent child hardly speaks throughout the novel. He acts silently and brutally, always from physical strength rather than intellectual ability. He comes into his own once Jack has assumed government of the island, performing the tasks that in a 'real' society would be undertaken by a public executioner.

Maurice

A clown or court jester, who always acts stupidly in order to win the attention of the other boys, Maurice is a natural comic but plays no significant part in the issues of the novel.

The other characters in the novel, like the interchangeable twins Sam and Eric, or the reticent but terrified little boy Percival, play relatively minor roles, but Golding nevertheless sketches them in with a lively sense of detail.

Part 4

Hints for study

Points to select for detailed study

The first thing to think about when studying *Lord of the Flies* is: has William Golding merely written a lively adventure story about a group of schoolboys marooned on a desert island or has he tried to say something profound?

Most readers (particularly if they are studying *Lord of the Flies* at school, college or university) will recognise that the novel offers more than a well-told narrative, but for this very reason we want to guard against underestimating its effectiveness as a yarn. The economy of the language, the sensitivity of the characterisation and the quick pace at which the action moves all contribute to an outstandingly successful adventure tale. Many children have read *Lord of the Flies* at about the age they are enjoying Ballantyne's *The Coral Island*, Stevenson's *Treasure Island* or Ransome's *Swallows and Amazons*—all of which are mentioned in the text (see notes to Chapter 1). Do not inquire into the moral and philosophical complexities of Golding's work at the expense of appreciating his mastery of the adventure-story form. He has taken a classic situation—young boys coping alone with the excitements of an exotic island—and invested it with new life and original insights.

Having established that the novel works successfully as a piece of story-telling, we next need to decide what kind of tale it is. Some dictionary definitions may be helpful (from the *Concise Oxford Dictionary*):

> **Fable:** story, especially of supernatural character, not founded on fact ... thing only supposed to exist ... short story, conveying a moral or apologue

Lord of the Flies largely fits this definition, as we have seen in Part 3. Though the supernatural does not play a direct part in the story we see how the boys create a supernatural set of values out of their fears and fantasies. They start to imagine mysteries in their surroundings which— as Simon perceives—only really exist as extensions of themselves. A fable, however, as this definition makes clear, must have a moral (that is, a maxim or principle which illustrates the distinction between good and bad). Another word for such a story is 'apologue', from the Greek 'apologos', meaning 'fable'.

Allegory: narrative description of a subject under the guise of another which is suggestively similar

A fuller discussion of the allegorical significance of *Lord of the Flies* appears in Part 3, on pp.42–3. 'Allegory' is a useful word to have in mind from the start of our reading, so that we can question as we go along what each character and situation may represent in the allegorical scheme. The word 'allegory' may be compared with the Greek word 'agora', meaning 'assembly', an interesting detail when so much of Golding's novel is concerned with assemblies.

Now that we have thought about the general form of the novel and seen that it contains elements of a boys' adventure story, a fable and an allegory, we need to look at *particular themes*. In Part 3, on pp.36–42, we examined the philosophical implications of the novel. In any work of fiction that offers a moral view of life or which attempts to derive metaphysical conclusions from man's relationship with nature and the universe the reader has the final right of acceptance or rejection. In other words, there are no right answers to what Golding writes about. All we can do, as critics of his work, is try to understand what he is attempting to say. Whether we agree with it or not will depend on our own religious, moral and social views. An agnostic may well react to Golding's pessimism more sympathetically than a Moslem or a Christian, for whom the prospect of an after-life is bound to shape the attitude towards human existence. As readers we must try not to reject a novel because we may disagree with its point of view. Instead we need (*a*) to understand the culture that has produced the author; (*b*) to see if there are any circumstances in the novelist's life that may have affected his view of the world; (*c*) to see, in aesthetic terms, whether the novelist offers his view of life with integrity: does the novel hold together consistently, does it seem to substitute dramatic effects for genuine feeling, and does it convince us that its characters would have acted and behaved in the way they are shown to do?

Points (*a*) and (*b*) may entail a little reading outside the novel and cannot therefore be considered an essential part of our critical study. Anything crucial to our appreciation of *Lord of the Flies* should be obvious from the text of the novel itself. However, in Part 1 the few details mentioned about Golding's life and about the period in which he wrote his first novel should be useful background to reading *Lord of the Flies*.

Point (*c*) brings us to the central business of criticism, which is examination of the actual text. We need to look at plot, language and characterisation.

The plot

Is it well constructed? This means studying the sequence of incidents in the novel to see that they progress naturally one from the other. Notice, for example, how Simon's death is the natural culmination of his wandering away from the other boys to find his own quiet retreat. During one such excursion he encounters both the dead parachutist and the pig's head on the stick, and thus understands that both 'the beast' and 'the Lord of the Flies' are figments of the human imagination. In other words, plot and character (Simon's death as the result of his desire for peace and knowledge) are inextricably related, the one being the natural consequence of the other. There are no sub-plots and no illogicalities in the ordering of events, though some incidents, like the arrival and departure of the dead parachutist in a windstream, emphasise the artificiality of the tale. Golding arranges the actions without trying to pretend that they are naturalistic (that is, that they would actually happen in this sequence in 'real' life).

The language

What kind of English does Golding use? We need to look at the simplicity of the English, with one or two consciously elevated passages (for example, Simon's sea-burial). Why does Golding use such straightforward language? Presumably because he wants the child's world to come to us as a child would perceive it. Remember that the novel is widely read by young people as well as by adults. Notice the indications of class in the contrast between Ralph's and Piggy's speech. Notice, too, the use of a child's-eye-view vocabulary (for example, 'mountain' and 'spear' for 'hill' and 'stick').

Characterisation

What attempt is there to be psychologically credible? We need to comment on the explicitly psychological incidents—the emphasis on dreams or the fear of the dark, for example. This extends to particular conflicts of character, that between Ralph and Jack being the most important. Remember how age affects behaviour. Piggy seems middle-aged though he is only the same age as Ralph and Jack. All three of them acquire an aspect of authority and responsibility in relation to the less personable children, or the 'littluns', which they would not have the opportunity to display in 'normal' adult society where they would only be little boys with nothing serious to worry about. Golding, in other words, gives the leading characters some of the characteristics of adults while never forgetting that they are first and foremost children.

Do the main characters develop in the course of the novel? We need to look at Ralph, Jack, Simon and Piggy at various stages of the novel to see how they change. This will involve studying what happens to them in terms of incident (how, for example, Jack's discovery of the effect of painting his face gives him a new confidence, or how Ralph faces up to the challenges to his leadership), but it will also mean our discussing the phobias and inner feelings which gradually break through the educated outer layer that each boy possesses at the start of the novel.

What part does each character play in an allegorical interpretation of the novel? This is discussed in Part 3.

Suitable quotations for study

The best way of discussing the form of the novel, the plot, the language and the characterisation, and of dealing with the areas of interest suggested above, is to look as closely as possible at particular passages of the text. Many readers will regret having to choose only two or three passages of quotation for analysis, as no extract can fully do justice to the complexity of a good novel. By focusing on some detailed passages, however, the reader may well be able to understand how the novelist achieves his effects throughout the whole work. The best advice is for students to select their own quotations for discussion, as these will be the moments in the text to which they have responded most immediately and personally.

The allegorical, or fable, form of the novel

No single quotation will do justice to this since it is an accumulative achievement only properly realised when the whole work is in view. Some moments, however, may help to explain the allegorical side of the book because they make the point explicit. Here is an example from Chapter 4:

> The subsoil beneath the palm trees was a raised beach; and generations of palms had worked loose in this the stones that had lain on the sands of another shore. Roger stooped, picked up a stone, aimed, and threw it at Henry—threw it to miss. The stone, that token of preposterous time, bounced five yards to Henry's right and fell in the water. Roger gathered a handful of stones and began to throw them. Yet there was a space round Henry, perhaps six yards in diameter, into which he dare not throw. Here, invisible yet strong, was the taboo of the old life. Round the squatting child was the protection of parents and school and policemen and the law. Roger's arm was conditioned by a civilization that knew nothing of him and was in ruins.

The whole thesis of *Lord of the Flies* is miniaturised in this passage. We have the primeval setting ('generations of palms') and the sense of a constantly evolving nature ('stones that had lain on the sands of another shore'). Within these the novelist shows us how human society has developed a corresponding pattern of behaviour. Roger starts by throwing stones at Henry for something to do, but we perceive a struggle in his subconscious between a desire to hit Henry—it is no fun deliberately to miss a ready-made target—and the knowledge, which society has instilled in him, that it is wrong to cause hurt. The episode sums up the conflict between the moral sense of man and his inclination to do as he pleases. Golding freely uses terms like 'taboo', 'protection' and 'civilization' which have specific meanings in an anthropological context, thus underlining his intention to say something generally true about human nature in the form of a story.

Plot

By apposite selection of quotations we can see how skilfully Golding narrates his tale. A good example is the hunting of the sow which eventually becomes the Lord of the Flies. The episode is too long to quote in full, but by judicious selection from Chapter 8 we can see the way Golding moves from detail to detail, accumulating tension as he does so and intensifying at each stage his study of man's inner nature. The episode mirrors the rise of emotionalism at the expense of self-control which Golding intends to be one of the principal themes of the novel.

Mid-way through the chapter we find Jack saying, 'We'll hunt. I'm going to be chief.' In a few phrases we are given the enthusiastic response of the other hunters. Then they track a pig-trail and encounter the matriarchal sow 'sensuously enjoying the shadow under the trees'. The pastoral idyll breaks as the boys attack the pigs, chase the sow and slaughter it in bloodthirsty abandonment. The language moves swiftly and graphically, culminating in the solemn words, slightly biblical in their tone, 'The sow collapsed under them and they were heavy and fulfilled upon her.' This gravity sounds again when the boys mount the head of the pig and offer it as a 'Gift for the Darkness' (we can see now why this is the title of the chapter): 'The silence accepted the gift and awed them. The head remained there, dim-eyed, grinning faintly, blood blackening between the teeth.'

The prose conveys the idea of an impressively impersonal outside world ('The silence . . . awed them'), which converts the dead animal into something terrifying and strange. We can see how the alteration of one word can change the tone, for only a few lines later, when Simon comes across the pig, the head is 'grinning amusedly' rather than 'faintly'. It has become a less hideous apparition, though possibly, in its contempt for the human world, a more chastening one.

Another possible method for analysing Golding's facility as a story-teller or for observing the narrative pattern of the novel would be to look at different sections which deal with similar situations. We could, for example, study every occasion when the boys meet together with the authority of the conch. Each episode extends the implication of the one before and also darkens it.

Language and symbol

In order to show how certain images recur throughout the novel we have to select several examples, showing their interconnection. The images of mirage and shadow will serve as an example. What connection exists, we have to ask, between the first appearance in Chapter 1 of the various boys on the beach—leaping 'into visibility when they crossed the line from heat-haze to nearer sand' or stepping 'from mirage on to clear sand'—and the boys in Chapter 11—walking along a beach 'shimmering in the heat . . . the reef . . . lifted by mirage, floating in a kind of silver pool half-way up the sky'? What connection is there between the 'witch-like cry' of the bird in the first paragraph of the novel and the 'ululation' which sounds through the island as Ralph is hunted in the final pages? Ambiguities of sight and associations of sound can be linked up in the novel to show how a network of related images binds the work together, giving it a linguistic as well as a philosophic unity.

Specimen questions

We should always keep in mind that the success of Golding's novel results from its total lack of excess. Complex attitudes are contained in a severely economical form and language. Our response to any question should try to match Golding's own succinctness with a corresponding order and simplicity.

The following list of questions covers most of the points about which any student of *Lord of the Flies* is likely to be asked. They are intended to be supplementary to the questions raised in the first two sections of Part 4.

(1) *In what way does* Lord of the Flies *reflect the literary climate of the early 1950s?*

This will involve reading round the subject. A contemporary social history of England will be useful, plus any work by Albert Camus or Jean-Paul Sartre, as well as Graham Greene's novel *The End of the Affair* and Samuel Beckett's *Waiting for Godot*.

(2) *Does William Golding have a coherent philosophy?*

This will require an opening statement of what you think Golding's philosophical views are, followed by a demonstration of how he argues this in the novel. This will, therefore, lead into a discussion of the allegorical and fable elements in the novel, since these are the means by which the philosophy comes to us.

(3) *Does Golding believe in the existence of good or is his vision of human nature wholly pessimistic?*

In answering this we may need to consider the possible theological implications of the novel—in particular the Christian doctrine of Original Sin. We shall certainly have to emphasise Simon's character, and we ought to show how the boys manage to create a workable society before their inner fears start to destroy their sense of responsibility and reason.

(4) *What does the 'beast' represent?*

(5) *What does the Lord of the Flies represent?*

(6) *What does the dead parachutist represent?*

(7) *What does the island represent?*

To answer questions (4)–(7) we shall need to talk about the psychology of the novel and about the relationship of the boys to the adult world from which they have been taken.

(8) *Trace the development of the conflict between Ralph and Jack and discuss whether it illustrates a fundamental split between two warring sides in man.*

This problem will lead us into a discussion of characterisation in the novel. It will also mean exploring its allegorical intention. Any question to do with the characters in *Lord of the Flies* will require us to talk about them both as recognisable people whom we might encounter in actual experience and as embodiments of particular aspects of human nature.

(9) *Explain the meaning of Simon's confrontation with the Lord of the Flies in Chapter 8.*

A topic like this asks us to look very closely at a particular episode. We shall therefore probably need to quote extensively, with regard to the import of some quite small phrases. We must then place the passage under discussion into the wider philosophical context of the novel.

(10) *What is the significance of the arrival of the naval officer on the island?*

Some critics believe that the novel should have ended with the words 'trying to cry for mercy' two and a half pages from the end. We need to ask whether the arrival of the naval officer holds out hope that man's ill nature is not beyond saving. Does the rescue of the boys signify the triumph of good over evil or does it confirm the impossibility of man's redemption from evil, since the boys will now return to an adult world which has been established earlier in the novel as intrinsically bad?

(11) *What kind of language does Golding use?*

(12) *How well constructed is this novel?*

(13) *Does Golding create convincing characters?*

(14) *What are the main sources of imagery and symbol in the novel?*

These questions can be answered along the lines indicated earlier in Part 4 and also in Part 3.

(15) *What relevance has* Lord of the Flies *to us today?*

This will mean discussing the theories about human nature which the novel proposes and then showing the extent to which they have dated, being products of a particular mood in post-war European society. We will need to emphasise the importance of a twentieth-century writer trying to examine the moral character of man in a language acceptable to readers who may no longer possess the certainties of belief which characterised earlier periods of European intellectual history.

Part 5

Suggestions for
further reading

The text

Lord of the Flies was first published by Faber & Faber, London, 1954; a
paperback edition is published by the same firm.

Other works by William Golding

GOLDING, WILLIAM, *The Hot Gates, and other occasional pieces*. Faber
& Faber, London, 1965.

Criticism and relevant books

Any question asked about *Lord of the Flies* should be answerable by
studying the text of the novel alone. If any of the following critical books
are unobtainable it does not matter, but they offer some interesting
insights into Golding's achievement. A number of critical essays have
been written about the novel in various journals and magazines, but
none of them need be regarded as essential reading.

BALLANTYNE, R.M., *The Coral Island*, Edinburgh, 1858. (This is
available in a number of modern editions.)
HOBBES, THOMAS, *The Leviathan, or the Matter, Form, and Power of a
Commonwealth, Ecclesiastical and Civil*. London, 1651. (This is
available in modern editions.)
HYNES, SAMUEL LYNN, *William Golding*, Columbia Essays on Modern
Writers, No. 2. Columbia University, USA, 1964.
KINCEAD-WEEKES, MARK, and GREGOR, IAN, *William Golding: A
Critical Study*. Faber & Faber, London, 1967.
MEDCALF, STEPHEN, *William Golding*, in the Writers and their Work
series, No. 243. Longman, Harlow, for the British Council, 1975.
PEMBERTON, CLIVE, *William Golding*, in the Writers and their Work
series, No. 210. Longman, Harlow, for the British Council, 1969.
TALON, HENRI A., *Le Mal dans l'oeuvre de William Golding* (in French).
Archives des Lettres Modernes, No. 73, Paris, 1966.

TIGER, VIRGINIA, *William Golding: The Dark Fields of Discovery*. Calder and Boyars, London, 1974.

WHITLEY, JOHN S., Golding's *'Lord of the Flies'*. Studies in English Literature, No. 42. Edward Arnold, London, 1970.

The author of these notes

Alastair Niven was educated at the Universities of Cambridge, Ghana and Leeds. He was a lecturer in the University of Ghana (1968–9), the University of Leeds (1969–70) and the University of Stirling (1970–8) before taking up his present position as Director-General of the Africa Centre, London. He is an honorary lecturer in the University of London.

His publications include *D. H. Lawrence: the novels*; and *The Yoke of Pity: the fiction of Mulk Raj Anand*. His *Truth into fiction: Raja Rao's 'The Serpent and the Rope'* is forthcoming. He has edited *The Commonwealth Writer Overseas*, and is co-editor of *The Journal of Commonwealth Literature*. He is writing *A History of Commonwealth Literature* for the Macmillan Histories of Literature. He has contributed to various books and written articles, mainly on Commonwealth literature, in scholarly journals.

York Notes: list of titles

CHINUA ACHEBE
A Man of the People
Arrow of God
Things Fall Apart

EDWARD ALBEE
Who's Afraid of Virginia Woolf?

ELECHI AMADI
The Concubine

ANONYMOUS
Beowulf
Everyman

JOHN ARDEN
Serjeant Musgrave's Dance

AYI KWEI ARMAH
The Beautyful Ones Are Not Yet Born

W. H. AUDEN
Selected Poems

JANE AUSTEN
Emma
Mansfield Park
Northanger Abbey
Persuasion
Pride and Prejudice
Sense and Sensibility

HONORÉ DE BALZAC
Le Père Goriot

SAMUEL BECKETT
Waiting for Godot

SAUL BELLOW
Henderson, The Rain King

ARNOLD BENNETT
Anna of the Five Towns

WILLIAM BLAKE
Songs of Innocence, Songs of Experience

ROBERT BOLT
A Man For All Seasons

ANNE BRONTË
The Tenant of Wildfell Hall

CHARLOTTE BRONTË
Jane Eyre

EMILY BRONTË
Wuthering Heights

ROBERT BROWNING
Men and Women

JOHN BUCHAN
The Thirty-Nine Steps

JOHN BUNYAN
The Pilgrim's Progress

BYRON
Selected Poems

ALBERT CAMUS
L'Etranger (The Outsider)

GEOFFREY CHAUCER
Prologue to the Canterbury Tales
The Franklin's Tale
The Knight's Tale
The Merchant's Tale
The Miller's Tale
The Nun's Priest's Tale
The Pardoner's Tale
The Wife of Bath's Tale
Troilus and Criseyde

ANTON CHEKHOV
The Cherry Orchard

SAMUEL TAYLOR COLERIDGE
Selected Poems

WILKIE COLLINS
The Moonstone
The Woman in White

SIR ARTHUR CONAN DOYLE
The Hound of the Baskervilles

WILLIAM CONGREVE
The Way of the World

JOSEPH CONRAD
Heart of Darkness
Lord Jim
Nostromo
The Secret Agent
Victory
Youth and *Typhoon*

STEPHEN CRANE
The Red Badge of Courage

BRUCE DAWE
Selected Poems

WALTER DE LA MARE
Selected Poems

DANIEL DEFOE
A Journal of the Plague Year
Moll Flanders
Robinson Crusoe

CHARLES DICKENS
A Tale of Two Cities
Bleak House
David Copperfield
Great Expectations
Hard Times
Little Dorrit
Nicholas Nickleby
Oliver Twist
Our Mutual Friend
The Pickwick Papers

EMILY DICKINSON
Selected Poems

JOHN DONNE
Selected Poems

THEODORE DREISER
Sister Carrie

GEORGE ELIOT
Adam Bede
Middlemarch
Silas Marner
The Mill on the Floss

T. S. ELIOT
Four Quartets
Murder in the Cathedral
Selected Poems
The Cocktail Party
The Waste Land

J. G. FARRELL
The Siege of Krishnapur

GEORGE FARQUHAR
The Beaux Stratagem

WILLIAM FAULKNER
Absalom, Absalom!
As I Lay Dying
Go Down, Moses
The Sound and the Fury

HENRY FIELDING
Joseph Andrews
Tom Jones

F. SCOTT FITZGERALD
Tender is the Night
The Great Gatsby

E. M. FORSTER
A Passage to India
Howards End

ATHOL FUGARD
Selected Plays

JOHN GALSWORTHY
Strife

MRS GASKELL
North and South

WILLIAM GOLDING
Lord of the Flies
The Inheritors
The Spire

OLIVER GOLDSMITH
She Stoops to Conquer
The Vicar of Wakefield

ROBERT GRAVES
Goodbye to All That

GRAHAM GREENE
Brighton Rock
The Heart of the Matter
The Power and the Glory

THOMAS HARDY
Far from the Madding Crowd
Jude the Obscure
Selected Poems
Tess of the D'Urbervilles
The Mayor of Casterbridge
The Return of the Native
The Trumpet Major
The Woodlanders
Under the Greenwood Tree

L. P. HARTLEY
The Go-Between
The Shrimp and the Anemone

NATHANIEL HAWTHORNE
The Scarlet Letter

SEAMUS HEANEY
Selected Poems

ERNEST HEMINGWAY
A Farewell to Arms
For Whom the Bell Tolls
The African Stories
The Old Man and the Sea

GEORGE HERBERT
Selected Poems

HERMANN HESSE
Steppenwolf

BARRY HINES
Kes

HOMER
The Iliad

ANTHONY HOPE
The Prisoner of Zenda

GERARD MANLEY HOPKINS
Selected Poems

WILLIAM DEAN HOWELLS
The Rise of Silas Lapham

RICHARD HUGHES
A High Wind in Jamaica

THOMAS HUGHES
Tom Brown's Schooldays

ALDOUS HUXLEY
Brave New World

HENRIK IBSEN
A Doll's House
Ghosts
Hedda Gabler

HENRY JAMES
Daisy Miller
The Europeans
The Portrait of a Lady
The Turn of the Screw
Washington Square

SAMUEL JOHNSON
Rasselas

BEN JONSON
The Alchemist
Volpone

JAMES JOYCE
A Portrait of the Artist as a Young Man
Dubliners

JOHN KEATS
Selected Poems

RUDYARD KIPLING
Kim

D. H. LAWRENCE
Sons and Lovers
The Rainbow
Women in Love

CAMARA LAYE
L'Enfant Noir

HARPER LEE
To Kill a Mocking-Bird

LAURIE LEE
Cider with Rosie

THOMAS MANN
Tonio Kröger

CHRISTOPHER MARLOWE
Doctor Faustus
Edward II

ANDREW MARVELL
Selected Poems

W. SOMERSET MAUGHAM
Of Human Bondage
Selected Short Stories

J. MEADE FALKNER
Moonfleet

HERMAN MELVILLE
Billy Budd
Moby Dick

THOMAS MIDDLETON
Women Beware Women

THOMAS MIDDLETON and WILLIAM ROWLEY
The Changeling

ARTHUR MILLER
Death of a Salesman
The Crucible

JOHN MILTON
Paradise Lost I & II
Paradise Lost IV & IX
Selected Poems

V. S. NAIPAUL
A House for Mr Biswas

SEAN O'CASEY
Juno and the Paycock
The Shadow of a Gunman

GABRIEL OKARA
The Voice

EUGENE O'NEILL
Mourning Becomes Electra

GEORGE ORWELL
Animal Farm
Nineteen Eighty-four

JOHN OSBORNE
Look Back in Anger

WILFRED OWEN
Selected Poems

ALAN PATON
Cry, The Beloved Country

THOMAS LOVE PEACOCK
Nightmare Abbey and *Crotchet Castle*

HAROLD PINTER
The Birthday Party
The Caretaker

PLATO
The Republic

ALEXANDER POPE
Selected Poems

THOMAS PYNCHON
The Crying of Lot 49

SIR WALTER SCOTT
Ivanhoe
Quentin Durward
The Heart of Midlothian
Waverley

PETER SHAFFER
The Royal Hunt of the Sun

WILLIAM SHAKESPEARE
A Midsummer Night's Dream
Antony and Cleopatra
As You Like It
Coriolanus
Cymbeline
Hamlet
Henry IV Part I
Henry IV Part II
Henry V
Julius Caesar
King Lear
Love's Labour's Lost
Macbeth
Measure for Measure
Much Ado About Nothing
Othello
Richard II
Richard III
Romeo and Juliet
Sonnets
The Merchant of Venice
The Taming of the Shrew
The Tempest
The Winter's Tale
Troilus and Cressida
Twelfth Night
The Two Gentlemen of Verona

GEORGE BERNARD SHAW
Androcles and the Lion
Arms and the Man
Caesar and Cleopatra
Candida
Major Barbara
Pygmalion
Saint Joan
The Devil's Disciple

MARY SHELLEY
Frankenstein

PERCY BYSSHE SHELLEY
Selected Poems

RICHARD BRINSLEY SHERIDAN
The School for Scandal
The Rivals

WOLE SOYINKA
The Lion and the Jewel
The Road
Three Short Plays

EDMUND SPENSER
The Faerie Queene (Book I)

JOHN STEINBECK
Of Mice and Men
The Grapes of Wrath
The Pearl

LAURENCE STERNE
A Sentimental Journey
Tristram Shandy

ROBERT LOUIS STEVENSON
Kidnapped
Treasure Island
Dr Jekyll and Mr Hyde

TOM STOPPARD
Professional Foul
Rosencrantz and Guildenstern are Dead

JONATHAN SWIFT
Gulliver's Travels

JOHN MILLINGTON SYNGE
The Playboy of the Western World

TENNYSON
Selected Poems

W. M. THACKERAY
Vanity Fair

DYLAN THOMAS
Under Milk Wood

EDWARD THOMAS
Selected Poems

FLORA THOMPSON
Lark Rise to Candleford

J. R. R. TOLKIEN
The Hobbit
The Lord of the Rings

CYRIL TOURNEUR
The Revenger's Tragedy

ANTHONY TROLLOPE
Barchester Towers

MARK TWAIN
Huckleberry Finn
Tom Sawyer

VIRGIL
The Aeneid

VOLTAIRE
Candide

EVELYN WAUGH
Decline and Fall
A Handful of Dust

JOHN WEBSTER
The Duchess of Malfi
The White Devil

H. G. WELLS
The History of Mr Polly
The Invisible Man
The War of the Worlds

ARNOLD WESKER
Chips with Everything
Roots

PATRICK WHITE
Voss

OSCAR WILDE
The Importance of Being Earnest

TENNESSEE WILLIAMS
The Glass Menagerie

VIRGINIA WOOLF
To the Lighthouse

WILLIAM WORDSWORTH
Selected Poems

W. B. YEATS
Selected Poems